THE GOD OF THE BIBLE
Logical, Evidential, Historical Proofs

Daniel Mann

THE GOD OF THE BIBLE
Logical, Evidential, Historical Proofs

Copyright 2021 by Daniel Mann

Printed in the United States of America

The Bible versions used in this publication are:

Daniel Mann, front cover photo
Anita Mann, back cover photo

Daniel Mann, author
Van Misheff, editor

Other books by Daniel Mann, edited by Van Misheff:

PRAYER: Confronting the Confusion
THEOLOGY: Reclaiming the Relevance
SCRIPTURE: Quest for Understanding

THANKS

First…
I thank the Lord
from whom comes all truth and wisdom.

Next…
I thank my wife
who has been my greatest fan and encouragement.

Last…
I thank my old friend and seminary buddy, Van Misheff,
who has carefully and faithfully edited this
and three other books for me.

TABLE OF CONTENTS

PART II
THE FRUITS OF CHRISTIANITY

5

INTRODUCTION

I thank God for my weaknesses. I had long been plagued with doubts. They were so destabilizing that I was unable to praise God or to live for Him in any confident manner. For example, I had been plagued with depression and self-loathing for decades. After a short honeymoon-period in the Faith, my old debilitating mind-set returned. I therefore concluded that if God did love me, He didn't love me very much. I even began to doubt whether I would ultimately end up in heaven.

Tormented, I searched for answers in the only place that I could— the Scriptures. I had already tried a host of different lifestyles, philosophies, self-help endeavors, and traveling. In addition, I had endured a broad array of psychotherapies, each one leaving me worse off than I was before. God was my last resort. If He didn't help me, I knew that there was no other recourse.

However, through my tormenting struggles, God has given me the clarity and the assurances that I needed. Now, I am thrilled to be able to pass on what I have received. This book is one result.

Daniel

EDITOR'S NOTE

It is always a privilege and a joy to edit Daniel's books. I can describe the work I do with my friend in seven simple words: "All I do is polish the gold."

❖ ❖ ❖

And now, some helpful details and specifics about this book:

Daniel is first and foremost a teacher. I write this so that the reader will not be surprised by a few instances of personal stories, illustrations from Scripture, or quotations that are repeated. This is what teachers do. They repeat, to emphasize that which is important.

As far as abbreviations are concerned, most of them should be clearly delineated in the book. For example, ID stands for Intelligent Design. Other, more common examples would be OT and NT, standing for the Old and New Testaments.

Some readers may notice that, in the "CITATIONS" section, there are instances when—although the quotation is accurate—a page number is not listed. It is sometimes very difficult to ascertain page numbers when doing research on-line. We did the best we could.

Finally, I am very grateful for the contributions of my friends:

Sam Cullado, who prepared the manuscript for Kindle;
Craig McSparran, who helped with formatting the manuscript;
and Rob Thomas, who proof-read the manuscript.

I pray that those who read this book will be strengthened in their faith.

Van

Chapter 1

PART I
NON-BIBLICAL PROOFS
FOR THE BIBLICAL GOD

DO WE REALLY NEED
THEISTIC AND CHRISTIAN PROOFS?

CHAPTER SUMMARY

Many churches teach that the mind and the fruits of mental inquiry simply get in the way of what we are called upon to do—to believe and to have faith. They speculate that the more we depend upon reason, the less we depend upon faith, the mainstay of the Christian life.

However, this does not reflect the Gospel that Jesus taught. Instead, He discouraged blind faith:

- "If I am not doing the works of my Father, then do not believe me; but if I do them, even though you do not believe me, *believe the works, that you may know and understand that the Father is in me and I am in the Father.*" (John 10:37-38; cf. John 5:31-38)

Jesus never suggested that we should quiet our minds; instead, He encouraged us to use our minds in our service to Him:

- And he said to him, "You shall love the Lord your God with all your heart and with all your soul *and with all your mind.* This is the great and first commandment." (Matthew 22:37-38)

Using our minds for godly service is part of the greatest commandment. However, our minds must first be convinced that the risen Christ is the truth. This was Jesus' strategy when He encountered His two disheartened disciples on the Emmaus Road.

After having seen the Crucifixion, they made this sad confession:

- "But we had hoped that he was the one to redeem Israel." (Luke 24:21a)

Jesus wanted to fill their hearts with confidence in the truth. He did this by reasoning from the Scriptures, the very thing they so desperately needed:

- And he said to them, "O foolish ones, and slow of heart to believe all that the prophets have spoken! Was it not necessary that the Christ should suffer these things and enter into his glory?" *And beginning with Moses and all the Prophets, he interpreted to them in all the Scriptures the things concerning himself.* (Luke 24:25-27)

These two discouraged disciples first needed to be humbled and shown that they had been taken captive by discouragement because they were not abiding in the Word. Then, Jesus provided them with tangible evidence from the Scriptures that the Crucifixion was actually a fulfillment of prophecy. Their eyes were opened. Now they could understand that—not only the Crucifixion, but also the Resurrection—had been clearly prophesied.

The assured knowledge of the truth energized these two disciples. The knowledge of the truth can energize us today as well. We need evidential reassurance for our faith, just like the disciples of old needed it. These newly-motivated believers returned immediately to Jerusalem and told the others what they had seen and heard from the Lord.

Now, let me try to anticipate your challenge:

- "Jesus was able to provide the best proofs of all—miracles. We cannot provide that kind of proof. Instead, our proofs can only provide us with a probability of the truths of God and not the assurance that we need."

Chapter 1

This, of course, is true. The proofs that I will be presenting may not be able to do much more than show that Christianity is superior to other worldviews and *probably* true. But this knowledge can certainly help us to counteract doubt. Proofs and apologetics, in general, serve as a protective shield surrounding the inner core of our faith. Without this shield, we are defenseless to protect our confidence in the Biblical faith, especially in light of the barbed arrows of doubt and uncertainty that constantly assail us.

Many have strayed from the faith in the absence of supporting rational answers. In *Search for the Truth*, Bruce Malone wrote:

- Prior to graduation from college, I had not once been shown any of the scientific evidence for creation either in school or in church. Little wonder, that by the time I started my career [as a chemist], God had little relevance in my life. It wasn't as though I had any animosity toward God or religion. It simply held no relevance to the world around me. This should be no surprise when the subject never came up in school and everything seemed to be explained without reference to a Creator.[1]

It is imperative that we believers know and embrace the supporting rational proofs for our faith.

❖ ❖ ❖

Apologetics is also helpful for cultural interaction. My apologetics professor at Trinity Evangelical Divinity School, William Lane Craig, stated that people will not believe what they regard as unbelievable. Today, many deem the Christian faith precisely that— "unbelievable." I think that part of the reason for this is that the Church has become intellectually lazy and compromised. We have lost the ability to show forth the wisdom and relevance of God in the public sphere. We are no longer as culturally proactive as we ought to be:

- The teaching of the wise is a fountain of life, turning a man from the snares of death. (Proverbs 13:14)

Chapter 1

Wisdom is part of our inheritance. We Christians have wisdom regarding so many areas of life—forgiveness, morality, justice, marriage, child-rearing and more. However, we have hidden our light under a bushel basket. Why? For one thing, we have failed to develop the ability to understand and critique the ideas of the world (2 Corinthians 10:4-5). As a consequence, we don't know how to apply the Gospel to the way the world thinks. Furthermore, we know this is true. Therefore, we fear the world, its challenges, and our interactions with it. What we need to do is learn to perceive the absolute poverty of the thinking that governs the world. Then we will not be driven to take cover.

Reasoning from the evidence matters, and God uses evidence to save. The late defender of the Christian faith and Oxford professor C.S. Lewis wrote in favor of theism, the belief in God:

- Nearly everyone I know who has embraced Christianity in adult life has been influenced by what seemed to him to be at least probable arguments for Theism. Even quite uneducated people who have been Christians all their lives not infrequently appeal to some simplified form of the Argument from Design.[2]

This doesn't mean that we are saved through a good argument. Instead, Lewis' observations testify to the fact that *God uses evidence to save and build His Church*. In fact, the Bible records many instances of this:

- He [Jesus] presented himself alive to them after his suffering *by many proofs*, appearing to them during forty days and speaking about the kingdom of God. (Acts 1:3)

Many people tell me, "I just know what I believe and nothing will change that." I am troubled by this answer. It suggests that people like this think that they are able to stand without the full armor that our Lord requires us to wear. If we are not careful, we can become smug, relying on ourselves for what we think we need to live. In stark contrast, the Apostle Paul warned:

- Therefore let anyone who thinks that he stands take heed lest he fall. (1 Corinthians 10:12)

Remembering the abject failure of the Israelites, Paul warned the Corinthians about the danger of thinking that they had no need to learn. They were convinced that the sins of Israel could never overtake them. Instead, they thought that they would stand simply because they were determined to stand.

❖ ❖ ❖

Before we go any further, let me ask a question: Is weighing evidence and proofs for the faith part of the full armor that God has prescribed for us? Are apologetics and the arguments for the Christian worldview part of the Biblically-prescribed armor—the "belt of truth" and the "shield of faith," found in Ephesians 6:15-16?

Some would argue that it is enough for us to know the Gospel without being cognizant of the challenges that come against it. This is not the message we find in Scripture. In the Bible, there are a number of admonitions warning us to be knowledgeable about false teachings:

- "*Beware of false prophets*, who come to you in sheep's clothing, but inwardly they are ravenous wolves." (Matthew 7:15)

- Then He charged them, saying, "Take heed, *beware of the leaven of the Pharisees and the leaven of Herod*." (Mark 8:15)

- *Beware lest anyone cheat you through philosophy and empty deceit*, according to the tradition of men, according to the basic principles of the world, and not according to Christ. (Colossians 2:8)

- Dear friends, do not believe every spirit, but test the spirits to see whether they are from God, *because many false prophets have gone out into the world*. (1 John 4:1)

However, it is not enough to be knowledgeable about the viper's venom after we have been bitten. We must understand it well enough to apply the right antidote. Likewise, it is not enough to simply avoid false teachings—*we are to proactively react and engage with them*. Any argument or idea that challenges the "knowledge of God" must be confronted. We must be able to show the wisdom of choosing ways of thinking and being that conform with Scripture:

- For the weapons of our warfare are not of the flesh, but divinely powerful for the destruction of fortresses. We are destroying speculations and every lofty thing raised up against the knowledge of God, *and we are taking every thought captive to the obedience of Christ*. (2 Corinthians 10:4-5)

For example, we are being told that God does not exist, that what we believe is an unnecessary and unsupportable myth. Furthermore, this myth has been made irrelevant by science, which claims to be able to contribute answers that religion once provided.

Even if we do not feel threatened by allegations like these, our children will feel threatened and will demand answers. If the Church is unable to provide them, our children will conclude that there are no answers and that the atheists are correct.

Like many others, I need to reassure myself in times of doubt and spiritual attack that I am going in the right direction. Theistic proofs, although they are unable to totally "seal the deal," have reassured me again and again that my Bible-centered beliefs and experiences are valid.

The limitations of these kinds of proofs should not discourage us. *All proofs are limited*. When I am dialoguing with an atheist who will not listen to any of the evidence that I provide, I simply turn the tables on him:

- "I would be glad to give you many proofs for the existence of God. However, since I don't talk to machines and computers, first simply prove that you exist. Then I will tell you everything you want to know."

The thoughtful atheist will soon realize that he too is unable to prove—absolutely—that he exists. Therefore, he should recognize that he is being unreasonable to demand that I absolutely prove that God exists. However, this does not mean that he will admit this to me. In fact, many atheists believe that they are little more than wet machines, even denying that we have free will.

❖   ❖   ❖

I don't think that any of us are above doubting. While in jail, John the Baptist began to doubt that Jesus was the One that he had publicly acknowledged Him to be—"the Lamb of God who takes away the sin of the world." He therefore sent his disciples to Jesus to confirm if He truly was the promised Messiah. Jesus did not answer John's delegation, as many might today, with a simple imperative: "Just tell John to believe." Instead, He provided His struggling prophet with evidential proof:

- And Jesus answered them, "Go and tell John what you hear and see: the blind receive their sight and the lame walk, lepers are cleansed and the deaf hear, and the dead are raised up, and the poor have good news preached to them." (Matthew 11:4-5)

We should notice here that Jesus did not perform a miracle for John in his cell. Instead, He gave John's disciples *eyewitness evidence* that they could convey to the jailed baptizer. This is exactly what we have today—a Bible filled with eyewitness evidence of the proofs for the Christian faith.

Chapter 1

Like John the Baptist, we too will find it necessary to seek out confirmation and reassurance for our faith. We can find all the assurance we need in the Bible. This accumulated body of evidence has served as powerful encouragement and confirmation for millions. It is only with these evidences that we can begin to fulfill our calling:

- Beloved, although I was very eager to write to you about our common salvation, I found it necessary to write appealing to you *to contend for the faith that was once for all delivered to the saints*. (Jude 3; 1 Peter 3:15)

To ignore such teachings is to refuse the command of God to love Him with all of our heart, soul, *and mind*. If we neglect to bring our minds to bear in this process, we leave the Church without defense. In this book, I hope to pass along valuable arguments for the defense of the faith—tools that have been indispensable for me.

Chapter 2

WHAT HAPPENS WHEN WE LOSE INTEREST IN TRUTH AND THE CHRISTIAN WORLDVIEW?

CHAPTER SUMMARY

What happens when Christians embrace Christ as Someone who has changed their lives and bestowed many benefits, and yet Christianity is not considered to be the truth? With this mind-set, we will falter, along with the Church.

What happens when Christians embrace Christ without believing that Christianity is *the* truth? In his essay, "Why Christianity Lost America," Indian scholar-turned-Christian, Vishal Mangalwadi, asks:

- Why did Christianity lose the power that gave it influence over education and economy, government and law, press and entertainment? How can the Church recover the power to prevail over the forces of evil?[1]

He goes on to explain that today's Christianity is not the vibrant Christianity of the recent past. Today's version believes that the idea of truth may be conveniently divorced from faith. Such an iteration of Christianity would leave her severely unbalanced—a plane with just one wing trying to fly with only feelings, mystical experiences, and a private and personalized faith— lethally separated from its Biblical and potently defensible truth-claims:

- Christianity lost America because 20th-century evangelicalism branded itself as the party of faith. By default, Secularism (science, university, media) became the party of truth. This is one reason why 70% of Christian youth give up meaningful involvement with the church when they grow up.[2]

Mangalwadi observes that many of today's Christians believe in a Christianity that has little to do with truth and facts. This

17

indefensible imbalance has proven to be disastrous for the Christian faith. Mangalwadi cites several examples:

- In November 2011, I met an American missionary who has served in Guatemala for 36 years. He described a recent (unpublished) doctoral study examining Protestantism in one part of Guatemala. The Hispanic scholar had hoped to substantiate Max Weber's thesis on the connection between Protestantism and economic development. The data, however, drove him to conclude that the gospel taught by present-day American missions makes no perceptible difference to the economic life of the believing communities.[3]

What a contrast with what Christianity has been historically!

One compelling example of the vibrancy of the Christian faith in America can be found in its establishment of universities. Sociologist Alvin Schmidt writes:

- Given the powerful influence that secularism now has on most Americans, they are probably not aware that "every collegiate institution founded in the colonies prior to the Revolutionary War—except the University of Pennsylvania—was established by some branch of the Christian church." Nor are most Americans aware that in 1932, when Donald Tewksbury published *The Founding of American Colleges and Universities before the Civil War*, 92 percent of the 182 colleges and universities were founded by Christian denominations.[4]

This should not surprise us. The Bible's teachings unequivocally testify that the Christian faith rests upon the undeniable truths of God (Deuteronomy 4:34-37)—what He has revealed and accomplished historically. God never asked Israel to believe without evidence. For example, when Moses asked God for evidence that he could share with the Israelites to prove that God had appeared to him, God did not say, "Well, just tell those

Israelites to believe!" Instead, He consistently provided the necessary proofs:

- Then Moses answered and said, "But suppose they will not believe me or listen to my voice; suppose they say, 'The LORD has not appeared to you.'?" So the LORD said to him, "What is that in your hand?" He said, "A rod." And He said, "Cast it on the ground." So he cast it on the ground, and it became a serpent; and Moses fled from it. Then the LORD said to Moses, "Reach out your hand and take it by the tail" (and he reached out his hand and caught it, and it became a rod in his hand), *"that they may believe that the LORD God of their fathers, the God of Abraham, the God of Isaac, and the God of Jacob, has appeared to you."* (Exodus 4:1-5)

Likewise, Jesus never instructed His followers to believe *without reasons to believe*. Instead, He provided copious evidence through His miracles and prophecies:

- He also presented Himself alive after His suffering *by many infallible proofs*, being seen by them during forty days and speaking of the things pertaining to the kingdom of God. (Acts 1:3)

- "You heard me say, 'I am going away and I am coming back to you.' If you loved me, you would be glad that I am going to the Father, for the Father is greater than I. *I have told you now before it happens, so that when it does happen you will believe.*" (John 14:28-29)

The Biblical faith embodies verifiable truths (1 Timothy 2:4; 2 Timothy 2:25; Titus 1:1). Mangalwadi contrasts this with other religions:

- Hinduism, like Greco-Roman religions, is based (self-consciously) on myths.

- The Buddha rejected Hinduism's mythical gods and goddesses in favor of mystical (non-rational) Silence.

- Islam has words that are believed to be true. These words were uttered in a state of non-rational trance, called "prophecy." Islam, therefore, rests on private, non-verifiable communications of an individual. Sometimes Mohammed went into "prophetic" trance in public, but no one saw or heard angel Gabriel talking to him. The power of his utterances rested on the sword, not on evidence. When his words about the past (e.g., stories from Old and New Testament times) contradicted documented history, his followers had to assume that contradictions mean that texts have been corrupted. Non-verifiable trance communications overrode documented history.[5]

Sadly, Christianity has been traveling down the same road as these other religions. In the face of secular attacks upon the truth-claims of Christianity, Christianity has retreated into a cocoon of private faith experiences. We have defensively responded with the now-familiar retort: "Well, I just know what I've experienced, and no one can tell me differently."

This response hasn't proven to be adequate. Against the weight of the claims of the modern university, Christianity has retreated and compromised. It has surrendered the life of the mind for the life of internal experiences. Mangalwadi explains:

- The church created the university to train godly leaders who [would] look at all of reality through the light of the Truth (revealed by God's works and words). Fundamentalism insulated Bible Institutes from other departments to study the Bible alone. It gave up the mission to seek public truth in favor of cultivating private spiritual lives. Once the Bible was put into the silo of Bible Institutes, the Bible teachers were isolated from the public life of the mind. Preachers memorized the Bible but by and large they did not learn how to meditate upon God's word in a way to shine its light on all of life.[6]

Chapter 2

We have compromised in many ways. We have put the claims of the Bible on the back-burner in favor of charismatic pastors. These men and women promise mountain-top experiences if we would only turn off our minds—if we would only stop insisting on checking out everything according to Scripture.

We have embraced a neo-orthodox, so-called "Christianity" that tries to salvage the Christian basics by insisting that the Bible really isn't about what it clearly teaches—historical truths. According to many, Christianity is strictly about spiritual truths, which are unconnected to the facts of history. On the contrary, the spiritual truths of the Bible depend upon its historical truths. For example, the spiritual truths we derive from Christ's suffering on the Cross depend upon the fact that He actually and historically died on the Cross.

Instead, we are being taught that the Bible is a tool that can magically bring us into a saving relationship with Christ, apart from its verifiable truth claims—claims that secular academics clearly reject. Why should we believe that God created the heavens and the earth? Why should we trust in the Biblical account of the Fall? According to certain religious "pundits," we can have Christ without any evidentially-based faith in the historical revelation of what He did.

❖   ❖   ❖

The Church has embraced theistic evolution in a vain attempt to make friends with the university and the "science" of our day. This worldview also attempts to make peace with that community by claiming that the Bible isn't so much about the physical world—science, history, and geography—as much as it is about the spiritual world. Therefore, according to this mind-set, there is no conflict between science and Christianity. How could there be? They exist in two totally separate realms.

However, in making this compromise, belief in theistic evolution has separated Christianity from all of its supporting evidence—the abundant, objective evidence all around us in the physical world.

Chapter 2

By accepting this false dichotomy between the spiritual and the physical world, Christians are relegated to a quasi-nether world—the realm of the spiritual—having abandoned the supportive evidences from history and science.

Real proof starts with what we know and can agree about—the physical world. Once this is established, it proceeds to the areas of disagreement—the spiritual claims. However, once the Church abandons the physical world, it no longer has an objective and shared basis to prove its case. As a consequence of this misguided thinking, some Christian leaders now describe themselves as "Christian Agnostics."

Many in the Church have embraced "Christian" mysticism and postmodern "Christianity." These have, in various ways, demeaned doctrine and apologetics in favor of experience, dogmatically claiming that we can't really know what is true with any degree of certainty. We are told that "doctrine divides," and that what really matters is a direct experience of God, apart from what we Biblically understand about Him. But how can people know what they are experiencing without the teachings of Scripture? Perhaps they are experiencing the deceptions of the demonic world (2 Corinthians 11:13-15).

Consequently, a number of Christians read the Bible mainly for *private* edification. Corporately, the Kingdom of Christ has ceased being "the city on a hill" or "the light of the world." Indeed, we cannot be the light if we believe that Biblical truth-claims are not verifiable. Moreover, we are now being justifiably scorned for following a "blind" faith.

In contrast to this, it was once widely accepted that the light of the Bible illuminated our relationship to God's creation. Because of this knowledge and light, we have been enabled to tame the natural world, lifting humanity and raising living standards for many:

- Modern science is an outgrowth of [the] Christian theology of the Middle Ages. It proceeded to show that it was Christianity's   values   that   provided   the

22

necessary *Weltanschauung* [worldview] and motivation to encourage many of its educated adherents to study the world of nature...The public are unaware that virtually all scientists from the Middle Ages to the mid-eighteenth century—many of which were seminal thinkers—not only were sincere Christians but were often inspired by Biblical postulates and premises in their theories...[they] knew and believed the words of the Biblical writer: "The heavens declare the glory of God; the skies proclaim the work of his hands." (Psalm 19:1)[7]

❖   ❖   ❖

What then is the answer for us today? To return with courage to the basics! Once again, Jesus instructed us to:

- "Love the Lord your God with all your heart and with all your soul *and with all your mind.*" (Matthew 22:37)

When we leave out truth and neglect the cultivation of the mind, we fail to live faithfully according to the teachings of Scripture. Instead, we distance ourselves and the world around us from the Scriptures and live defensively, fearful that we will be confronted with questions and challenges that we cannot answer. We therefore practice avoidance. Instead of being a light on a hill, we have abdicated our place, allowing the prevailing culture to be our light.

Once we lose confidence in the Light and Truth of Christ, we become indistinguishable from the world. We no longer have the conviction or the faith to live according to the teachings of the Bible. Eventually, the Bible begins to feel judgmental and legalistic. It is then inevitable that our affections will become set on the things of this world. (1 John 2:15-16; James 4:4)

Holistic assurance is only possible when the mind is engaged and assured. Let us therefore feast upon the many reasons to believe in God and in His Word!

Chapter 3

IS THE BIBLE
AT WAR AGAINST SCIENCE?

CHAPTER SUMMARY

Skeptics argue that we Christians cannot do science because our minds are already made up. However, skeptics also approach science with their own biased worldview—naturalism.

We've all heard these indictments against the role of religion and Christianity:

- "Science has been able to achieve so much for the world because it has not been tied down to religious commitments and ideas. Christians, on the other hand, approach science with presuppositions that make it impossible for them to deal impartially with the evidence. Therefore, Christianity, as well as the other religious traditions, should be kept out of science."

Although this statement might sound rational, there are many incorrect assumptions lurking behind these words. I will present the assumptions in **bold** and then the counter-arguments:

1. Christians and other "religious" people are the only ones who have presuppositions that might interfere with scientific inquiry.

All of us have presuppositions, values, philosophical commitments, and religious sentiments.

Even secular humanists used to refer to their belief system as a religion; that is, until they realized that they had more to gain by denying this fact. The Preface of the first Humanist Manifesto, written by atheist Paul Kurtz in 1933, openly declared: "Humanism is a philosophical, religious, and moral point of view." Therefore, the argument for removing religion from science should—according to this definition—apply as well to atheism.

24

Chapter 3

2. Christians can't do science.

This simply does not accord with the facts. The record of history highlights the great role that Christians played in the development of science. British scientist Robert Clark sums it up with this startling assertion:

- However we may interpret the fact, scientific development has only occurred in Christian culture. The ancients had brains as good as ours. In all civilizations—Babylonia, Egypt, Greece, India, Rome, Persia, China and so on— science developed to a certain point and then stopped. It is easy to argue speculatively that, perhaps, science might have been able to develop in the absence of Christianity, but in fact, it never did. And no wonder. For the non-Christian world believed that there was something ethically wrong about science. In Greece, this conviction was enshrined in the legend of Prometheus, the fire-bearer and prototype scientist who stole fire from heaven, thus incurring the wrath of the gods.[1]

3. The naturalistic explanations are the only ones that are scientific.

Recently, science has been hijacked by naturalism. This worldview believes, without any evidence, that the laws and materials of science are natural and without any intelligent causation. Therefore, the only explanations allowed among the vast majority of the scientific community are those that do not include ID, intelligent design.

However, this naturalistic assumption is highly problematic. It assumes that the natural laws just appeared, or, that they have always existed without any cause. And all of this supposedly occurred even before the existence of anything *natural* was present to explain the origin of the natural laws. It makes much more sense to acknowledge that there is one eternal, uncaused Causer who is more than adequate to explain all the phenomena of our cosmos.

Besides, there is not the slightest bit of experimental or observable evidence that proves that everything which happens is naturally caused. Furthermore, there is no evidence proving that ID is not involved in causation. But, since the naturalistic worldview now controls the scientific establishment, it is no longer academically or scientifically acceptable to question this so-called "truth."

While we cannot *scientifically* prove that either natural or supernatural causation is at work, there are nevertheless many reasons to regard the supernatural paradigm—intelligent design—as preferable.[2]

4. Christian presuppositions will take us in an unscientific direction.

This is totally unfounded. Instead, Christian scientists use the exact same experimental techniques as their non-Christian colleagues. In fact, specifically Christian presuppositions have played an essential role in recent scientific inquiry in the West. For example, since Christian scientists have long believed in creation-out-of-nothing, they were able to anticipate the major findings of Big Bang cosmology—that the universe had a beginning and a first cause.

In addition, the paradigm of Biblical creationism was able to anticipate the First and Second Laws of Thermodynamics. The First Law claims that matter/energy cannot be created or destroyed. Interestingly, this reflects the Biblical revelation that God stopped creating after the sixth day, while naturalism assumes gradual development.

The Second Law posits the reign of entropy, the gradual breakdown of complexity. This too is anticipated by the Biblical revelation of a "very good" creation and its subsequent breakdown as a result of the Fall. Naturalism assumes the very opposite thing—gradual progress and development.

Consistent with the naturalistic paradigm, evolutionary scientists were quick to embrace the ideas of "junk," or "leftover" DNA and vestigial organs. Organs deemed to be vestigial were supposed to be "leftovers" from evolutionary ancestors. The concepts of junk DNA and vestigial organs were both soundly embraced by most of the scientific community, since they were both compatible with evolutionary pre-suppositions. However, recent scientific findings have disposed of both of these theories.[3]

**5.	Naturalistic,	atheistic	presuppositions—those presuppositions that recognize no role for an intelligent Designer, God—are the most scientifically fruitful, since they are neutral and do not impede science.**

Instead, the truth is that *we all see through a pre-suppositional lens*. Once we recognize this foundational truth, the question then becomes, "Which lens brings reality into sharper focus, and which lens distorts our perception of reality?" C.S. Lewis wrote:

- I believe in Christianity as I believe in the sun—not only because I see it, but because by it I see everything else.[4]

According to Lewis, Christianity is the lens that brings everything else into focus. Let me try to give an example of this. In many ways, the Bible says that we are sin-infested, even the best of us (Romans 7:25; Galatians 5:17). This lens—though at times a painful "pill" to swallow—has enabled me to fruitfully navigate life's demands in so many ways.

On the surface, people might appear to be doing really well, but seeing life through the Christian lens has convinced me that there is no one who has truly "arrived." There are no enlightened gurus who have been able to fabricate a heaven on earth—there are only people like me. Seeing through this lens has enabled me to accept myself, knowing that the struggles I have are little different from those that others face. It has also helped me to accept others, despite how they might have disappointed me. I know as well that there is no one ultimately perfect Mrs. Right out there. Instead, each one of us comes into a relationship with a load of issues.

Chapter 3

DOES THE CHRISTIAN "LENS" PRODUCE SCIENTIFIC CLARITY?

In his debate with the ardent atheist Richard Dawkins, John Lennox stated that the scientific community should have taken seriously the Bible's assertion that God created the universe. If it had done so, it would probably have found evidence to reject the widely accepted Aristotelian idea of an eternal universe—the Steady State theory—much sooner.[5]

I think that there are many examples of this kind of thing. Here's another: A broad spectrum of evidence weighs in favor of *de-evolution* and the corrosion of our genome, as opposed to evolution and an improvement of our genome. Instead of natural selection performing a gradual "house-cleaning" to rid us of genetic defects, humanity is actually accumulating genetic defects. Also, rather than observing a proliferation of species, it is now generally agreed that 98% of all species on earth have disappeared. These findings fit the Biblical revelation. In the beginning, God made everything just right; but after the Fall, deterioration has followed.

Furthermore, I predict that much of the research to find the natural origins of RNA, DNA, the cell, and life itself—in its quest to disqualify ID—will merely drain us of a lot of money and time.

❖ ❖ ❖

It is apparent that naturalism cannot account for many observable facts. Most obviously, as I have already pointed out, naturalism cannot account for how the laws of science came about naturally. Nor can natural laws explain how they can affect everything in the universe, while nothing can affect them. Furthermore, how can these laws remain immutable in a universe of constant change? The laws of science cannot explain how an explosion—the Big Bang—could create our elegant and immutable laws. Repeated observation and experience tell us that explosions routinely create disorder and chaos—not laws—and certainly not universes.

Chapter 3

Is the Bible at war against science and its systematic observations? Not according to the Scriptures! The Bible calls us to observe the universe, God's creation, *as proof of its Creator:*

- For what can be known about God is plain to them, because God has shown it to them. *For his invisible attributes, namely, his eternal power and divine nature, have been clearly perceived, ever since the creation of the world, in the things that have been made.* So they are without excuse. (Romans 1:19-20)

Consistent with these verses, science has shown us that life is more than a haphazard amalgamation of jelly. Instead, it is a collection of cells, each containing an irreducibly complex array of machinery. Even the molecular components—proteins and DNA—are so complex and highly functional that, if they could, they would laugh at any naturalistic explanation of their origins. Here are several testimonies to this amazing fact:

- The cell is as complicated as New York City.[6]

- A bacterium is far more complex than any inanimate system known to man. There is not a laboratory in the world which can compete with the biochemical activity of the smallest living organism.[7]

The appearance of design, not only in biology but also in the cosmos itself, is so extensive that even atheists are forced to acknowledge it. However, their faith in science is tenacious. They claim that at this point in time, science might not have reasons and answers for consciousness or the fine-tuning of the universe, but eventually it will discover them!

Such a stance is no more than a leap of faith. In *Heretic: One Scientist's Journey from Darwin to Design*, award-winning Finnish biotechnologist, Matti Leisola, has written about his observations:

- Over and over again I have encountered materialist fanaticism from people who are not ready to give up their views in the face of contrary evidence. Actually, they usually are not even interested in considering the evidence.[8]

Why is it that scientists do not even consider any explanations that lie outside of their naturalistic/materialistic "box"? According to Leisola:

- ...most scientists who go along with methodological materialism put about as much thought into it as they do breathing. I was that way. And in hundreds of discussions over the years I have witnessed a blindness to basic philosophical commitments in many kinds of people from at least thirty different nationalities. Even among scientists few are aware of their basic presuppositions. Most of them consider science a neutral search for truth.[9]

The scientific community has become committed to naturalism, which religiously discounts a Designer in favor of only naturalistic, unintelligent causation. Meanwhile, there is absolutely no evidence to support the idea that *anything* has ever happened naturally, without intelligence. However, with a religious zeal they would never acknowledge, the vast bulk of the scientific community has stubbornly insisted that life has evolved from non-life. Leisola continues:

- The 1960 declaration of famous paleontologist George Gaylord Simpson in the journal *Science* is representative: "The consensus is that life did arise naturally from the nonliving and that even the first living things were not specially created," he wrote.[10]

Consensus is not the same as evidence. *There is no evidence whatsoever* that the cosmos or life is *not* designed. We therefore wonder, "How great a level of complexity, elegant functionality, and the appearance of design must be revealed before the naturalist will confess that a naturalistic explanation is no longer possible?"

Some ex-atheists have already reached that point.

Chapter 4

DOES SCIENCE PROVE GOD?

CHAPTER SUMMARY
The findings of biology and cosmology suggest that science has a lot to say about the existence of an intelligent Designer, as many scientists have affirmed.

Most atheists acknowledge that science cannot disprove God. At the same time, they claim that it would also be impossible for science to prove Him. Here is what they offer as the reason for their stance: "Your god is of the 'spiritual'—and therefore, unmeasurable—world; whereas, science deals only with that which is measurable." However, there are indications to the contrary.

If the sciences had revealed a world of chaos instead of order and design, I think that atheists and scientists would be able to discount the existence of an intelligent Designer. However, the findings of science tell us just what our senses have always told us—that the universe we inhabit could not possibly have been fashioned by chance. When we observe the world, we see order, design, complexity, functionality, harmony, and beauty. And all of these components tell us that this creation is the glorious invention of a Creator, just as Paul declared in Romans 1:19-20.

In fact, the sciences are discovering that even "chaos" has its order. Mathematician Ian Stewart succinctly stated that, "Chaos is lawless behavior governed entirely by law."[1]

Actually, this is a common observation in the sciences. No physical object is unaffected by or immune to the elegant and orderly laws of science. How can this be? Perhaps all we can say is that the world is indeed quite remarkably interrelated and integrated.

One primary example of this can be seen in the idea that matter cannot exist without time and space. Nor does it seem that time can exist without space and matter. Einstein's famous formula illustrates, in one small way, the extent of the interrelationship:

E (energy) = M (mass) x C^2 (the speed of light, *precisely* squared)

The order and relationships in this equation are precise, elegant, immutable, and universal. They work uniformly throughout the universe. They pertain to and are maintained changelessly throughout our changing and expanding universe. These considerations strongly suggest that the laws of science originate beyond the physical world and require some form of transcendent causation and upkeep.

Nor is it just Einstein's formula that bears the fingerprints of the Transcendent. This pertains to *all* of the formulas and causation discovered by science. All of them are elegant, immutable, universal, and remain unchanging in a messy world of continual change. Their reach is limitless. They uniformly and predictably touch everything in their inescapable path, while nothing from the material world is able to influence or change them. It is as if they come from Beyond...perhaps even from the all-wise mind of the Creator.

Science has shown us that life is more than random compounds of jelly called "cells." In fact, each cell contains an irreducibly complex array of machinery. Even the molecular components of the cellular world—proteins and DNA—are so complex and hyper-functional that any naturalistic explanation for how they came into being, or how they function, is inadequate. Even atheists acknowledge this cellular wonder-world:

- A living cell is a marvel of detailed and complex architecture. Seen through a microscope there is an appearance of almost frantic activity. On a deeper level it is known that molecules are being synthesized at an enormous rate. Almost any enzyme catalyzes the synthesis of more than 100 other molecules per second. In ten minutes, a sizeable fraction of total mass of a metabolizing bacterial cell has been synthesized. The information content of a simple cell has been estimated as around 10^{12} bits, comparable to about a hundred million pages of the Encyclopedia Britannica. Can these wonders be explained by mindless, uncaused, unassisted "natural" forces? Or is it more reasonable to infer the existence of an Intelligent Designer?[2]

❖ ❖ ❖

Science is shedding more and more light on the exquisite fine-tuning of the universe. Its constants have been calibrated with astounding precision to support life. In *Nature's Destiny: How the Laws of Biology Reveal Purpose in the Universe*, biologist Michael Denton wrote:

- As the eerie illumination of science penetrates ever more deeply into the order of nature, the cosmos appears increasingly to be a vast system finely tuned to generate life and organisms of biology very similar, perhaps identical, to ourselves. All the evidence available in the biological sciences supports the core proposition of traditional natural theology—that the cosmos is a specially designed whole with life and mankind as a fundamental goal and purpose, a whole in which all facets of reality, from the size of galaxies to the thermal capacity of water, have their meaning and explanation in this central fact. Four centuries after the scientific revolution apparently destroyed irretrievably man's special place in the universe, banished Aristotle, and rendered teleological speculation obsolete, the relentless stream of discovery has turned dramatically in favor of teleology and design, and the doctrine of the microcosm is reborn.[3]

According to Denton, science has provided powerful evidence "that the cosmos is a specially designed whole with life and mankind as a fundamental goal and purpose..." However, on a regular basis, we are being told that science has made God irrelevant. Textbook author and evolutionist Douglas Futuyma has written that Darwinism and the sciences have made spiritual explanations—that is, ID—irrelevant:

- Darwin showed that material causes are a sufficient explanation not only for physical phenomena, as Descartes and Newton had shown, but also for biological phenomena with all their seeming evidence of design and purpose. By coupling undirected, purposeless variation to the blind, uncaring process of natural selection, Darwin made theological or spiritual explanations of the life processes superfluous.[4]

This might seem true as long as science is content with superficial answers. However, that is not the case. Science has been asking questions about the creation of the universe and its laws:

✓ Can natural, un-designed causal forces explain the origins and nature of the universe?

✓ Is there one unifying, causal natural principle that can explain everything else?

✓ Can naturalism account for the elegant, immutable, and universal laws of science?

✓ Is there any evidence that anything has ever occurred naturally, without the application of intelligent design?

I think that the answer to all of these questions is a resounding "No"—which should put ID back on the discussion table.

❖ ❖ ❖

Meanwhile, naturalistic science is struggling to answer the great teleological questions, like the origin of life, DNA, and the cell. Physicist, philosopher, and professor at Arizona State University, Paul Davies, concluded that chance events could not account for what he had been observing:

- Scientists are slowly waking up to an inconvenient truth—the universe looks suspiciously like a fix. The issue concerns the very laws of nature themselves. For 40 years, physicists and cosmologists have been quietly collecting examples of all too convenient "coincidences" and special features in the underlying laws of the universe that seem to be necessary in order for life, and hence conscious beings, to exist. Change any one of them and the consequences would be lethal. The crucial point is that some of those metaphorical knobs (of which there are 40) must be tuned very precisely, or the universe would be sterile. Example: neutrons are just a tad heavier than protons. If it were the other way around, atoms couldn't exist, because all the protons in the universe would have decayed into neutrons shortly after the big bang. No protons, then no atomic nucleus and no atoms. No atoms, no chemistry, no life.[5]

The only other viable explanation for this fine-tuned universe is the multiverse. This theory claims that if there are an infinite number of universes, it is likely that one of them would be as fine-tuned as ours. However, many regard the multiverse as a desperate attempt to avoid God. Here's why:

✓ There is no evidence for a second universe, let alone an infinite number of them.

✓ If there were other universes out there with other sets of laws, what would keep them from interacting and undermining one another? Instead, it seems that an unlimited number of universes would make contact and corrupt the others.

✓ There is no known mechanism to generate other universes. Besides, a mechanism capable of generating a theoretically infinite number of universes would surely be no less complex than that which was needed to generate this one.

✓ It is also logically impossible. An infinite number of universes would require an infinite amount of time and space. However, if time always existed, it would be impossible to fulfill an infinite number of years to ever arrive at the present time.

British astrophysicist George Ellis sees the scientific evidence pointing to ID:

- Amazing fine tuning occurs in the laws that make this [complexity] possible. Realization of the complexity of what is accomplished makes it very difficult not to use the word 'miraculous' without taking a stand as to the ontological status of the word.[6]

Nobel Laureate in physics Arno Penzias came to the same conclusion:

- Astronomy leads us to a unique event, a universe which was created out of nothing, one with the very delicate balance needed to provide exactly the conditions required to permit life, and one which has an underlying (one might say 'supernatural') plan.[7]

Frank Tipler, Professor of Mathematical Physics, recounts:

- When I began my career as a cosmologist some twenty years ago, I was a convinced atheist. I never in my wildest dreams imagined that one day I would be writing a book purporting to show that the central claims of Judeo-Christian theology are in fact true, that these claims are straightforward deductions of the laws of physics as we now understand them. I have been forced into these conclusions by the inexorable logic of my own special branch of physics.[8]

From the scientific evidence, Tipler and the others mentioned above have concluded that naturalism cannot account for the facts. Only ID can.

I would go a step further. Even the exercise of science assumes and depends on the bedrock of the immutable, universal, and elegantly designed laws and forces of science. Without these wonderfully-designed and predictable laws, there could be no science at all. Consequently, the very fact that we can do science and accumulate knowledge depends on a God who has designed it all—the very God we stubbornly deny. We have moved into His home, tossed Him out, and have claimed His domain as our own.

❖ ❖ ❖

Why should we believe that these laws of science are supernatural, as opposed to natural? And what is it that immutably maintains these laws and forces in a world of molecules-in-motion?

Everything we observe cries out "design," even the smallest atom. Does science prove God? Science cannot utter a single syllable without God. All of its findings should be labeled, "Made by the Designer."

In fact, the evidence for a Designer is so compelling that many scientists are abandoning atheism as a failed hypothesis. Astronomer and former atheist Alan Sandage wrote:

- As I said before, the world is too complicated in all of its parts to be due to chance alone. I am convinced that the existence of life with all its order in each of its organisms is simply too well put together...The more one learns of biochemistry the more unbelievable it becomes unless there is some kind of organizing principle—an architect.[9]

The late atheist, Antony Flew, gives an account of how and why he concluded that DNA requires an intelligent cause. The following quotations are representative of his reasoning:

- It now seems to me that the findings of more than fifty years of DNA research have provided materials for a new and enormously powerful argument for design.[10]

- To the surprise of all present, I announced at the start [of a May 2004 symposium at New York University] that I now accepted the existence of a God...I now think it [the evidence] does point to a creative Intelligence almost entirely because of the DNA investigations. What I think the DNA material has done is that it has shown, by the almost unbelievable complexity of the arrangements which are needed to produce life, that intelligence must have been involved in getting these extraordinarily diverse elements to work together.[11]

Flew, who used to argue for atheism in debates against Professor C.S. Lewis, became a theist based upon the evidence of science. Meanwhile, science offers no evidence in favor of non-design, especially at science's most seminal levels. But if science offers no evidence against the existence of a Designer, why is His existence denied? Purely by choice!

To this, the atheist confidently responds: "Science has nothing to say about the non-existence of either the tooth fairy or the spaghetti-monster, nor should it."

This objection misses the point. The atheists' spaghetti-monster is irrelevant to science and existence, and everyone agrees. Instead, theists posit an eternal and uncaused Intelligent Designer as the most viable causal Agent to explain all else—moral law, consciousness, free will, the laws of science, the fine-tuning of the universe, and the myriad appearances of design.

Skeptics respond, "Well, the spaghetti-monster can do likewise. He too can serve as our Creator God!" However dismissive this response might be, it also acknowledges a Creator God, a single Cause that can explain all else without invoking a wide variety of "natural" causes to explain the same phenomena. The only thing that is changed here is the name. The skeptic has merely exchanged the name "God" for a laughable one—the "Spaghetti-Monster."

❖   ❖   ❖

Regarding ID, science is attempting to address a fundamental question of origin: Did the world come into existence out of nothing, by itself? Or was it designed by a transcendent Being? Furthermore, is it possible to confidently assume "natural" causation if the "natural" does not pre-exist what it is explaining?

Certainly germane to this discussion is the question: What does the flagship of naturalism—the theory of evolution—say about the Intelligent Designer, God? First, it must be freely acknowledged on both sides of this issue...that we all believe in change-over-time. Creationists believe that all of the human races and their variations came from a single couple. The widely diverse racial and ethnic groupings of humanity offer a clear illustration of these changes, over the course of time. We call this micro-evolution, the tiny changes that occur within species.

Macro-evolution is a different story. According to macro-evolution, all of the changes that occurred from the simple amoeba up to humans came about through natural and unguided forces. Does this mean that evolution has replaced God? Not at all! Even if macro-evolution did occur, science has not been able to offer one piece of evidence that it wasn't guided by God.

However, this is not the only problem with evolution. For one thing, as stated earlier, there is no evidence that *anything* has ever occurred or changed *naturally*, without design. In our universities, where naturalism reigns as the scientific alternative to the Creator God, this statement might sound extreme. Don't we talk about the "natural" laws of science? Of course we do! And we all agree that phenomena predictably and verifiably occur according to the operation of the laws and forces of science. However, the question we need to ask ourselves is this: "Do these laws originate and operate, and are they sustained *naturally*...or do they proceed from the mind of God?"

This is the very question we will address in the next chapter.

Chapter 5

FREE WILL
CAN BE CONSISTENTLY AFFIRMED
ONLY BY THEISM

CHAPTER SUMMARY

Free will cannot be denied without also denying our most basic perception of ourselves. There are also many other reasons to believe in free will. However, materialism and naturalism can provide no basis for free will…and therefore deny it. This denial is also the denial of civilization.

In 1871, Thomas Huxley, a zealous advocate of Charles Darwin, claimed that "Mind is nothing but matter." Of course, since matter is exclusively under the control of the laws of science, this understanding leaves no room for free will.

As far as the atheist Sam Harris, the author of *Free Will*, is concerned, "Free will is an illusion." Therefore, what feels like free will is nothing more than a combination of chemical processes. This perspective leaves no room for human culpability. In other words, none of us can be held responsible for anything we do. If our thoughts and actions are entirely controlled by biochemical reactions, then we actually don't have any choice about what we end up doing—we couldn't have acted otherwise. Hence, there is no basis for any culpability on our part, or even guilt.

However, this denial of free will and culpability, which I will refer to as DFC, is highly problematic for a number of reasons.

PROBLEMS ASSOCIATED WITH
THE DENIAL OF FREE WILL AND CULPABILITY

DFC goes against everything we intuitively know about ourselves and our lives.

When I make any decision, like flipping through the TV channels, it seems that I am freely choosing one station over another. Of course, like anyone else, I am subject to powerful biological-genetic forces. Admittedly, I am biologically predisposed to not like loud and glitzy programming. Therefore, some will say, "Well, this proves you're pre-programmed to make certain choices."

Although there is some truth in this claim, it falls far short of proving that a genetic pre-disposition is the *only* factor involved in my choices.

Of course, Harris and other atheists would respond that what I had thought to be an experience of free choice was in actuality an illusion. However, if something that I experience with such clarity is illusory, perhaps my very existence and the existence of the world are *also* illusory. Perhaps I'm just a figment of someone else's consciousness. Perhaps, as some Buddhists claim, we all are merely part of one universal consciousness and therefore lack any individual existence.

If our intuitions and perceptions are simply part of a great delusion, then *all of science and all reason would also be part of this same delusion.*

In other words, if I were to apply such skepticism to my perception that, to some degree, I am making culpable, free choices, then I would have to be skeptical about everything else in my life! I would even have to be skeptical about my skepticism.

To an extent, free will and culpability differ among people.

One proponent of DFC whom I know, claims that we cannot possess differing amounts of free will, since free will is *entirely* absent in each of us:

- "There are only two types of people in the world. Those who believe in free will and those who do not. There is no grey area or wiggle room…There is no such thing as a little free will."

Yet, it is clear that we do possess differing degrees of free will. For example, the heroin addict is more constrained in his free choices than he was before he became addicted. When he or she is actively using, he can think of little else besides his next fix.

And what about captives given a drug—LSD or truth serum—to control their behavior? Do they not have less freedom of choice and culpability than before? Or, what about those who are comatose? Or how about when someone puts a gun to our head, forcing us to commit a crime? Should we not take these individual considerations into account?

If we do possess varying degrees of free will, then the narrow, unvarying materialistic view which denies *any* area of free will and culpability is clearly mistaken. From the perspective of the deniers of free will, everyone is equally and completely controlled by brain chemistry. As a result, there can be no room for varying degrees of free will and culpability—the very distinctions upon which our justice system and our schools depend!

We can perceive a distinction
between the purely chemical determination
of our behavior and our relatively free responses.

Wilder Penfield (1891-1976), the father of modern neurosurgery, performed experiments demonstrating that brain activity does not seem to account for all of our mental experience. Lee Edward Travis sums up Penfield's findings this way:

- Penfield would stimulate electrically the proper motor cortex of conscious patients and challenge them to keep one hand from moving when the current was applied. The patient would seize this hand with the other hand and struggle to hold it still. Thus one hand under the control of the electrical current and the other hand under the control of the patient's mind fought against each other. Penfield risked the explanation that the patient had not only a physical brain that was stimulated to action but also a nonphysical reality that interacted with the brain.[1]

Chapter 5

There appears to be a distinction between brain chemistry and a nonphysical reality—where free will seems to reside. J.P. Moreland commented on another interesting aspect of Penfield's findings:

- No matter how much Penfield probed the cerebral cortex, he said, "There is no place...where electrical stimulation will cause a patient to believe or to decide."[2]

If our mind is no more than a physical brain, then we should expect that electrical charges could stimulate *every* kind of response. This is not the case. It seems that our choices and beliefs cannot be entirely accounted for by the physical brain.

There seems to be a nonphysical basis for thinking.

Raymond Moody published *Life after Life* in 1975, based upon 150 interviews with people who claimed to have had near-death experiences, or NDEs. Cardiologist and assistant professor at Emory University School of Medicine, Michael Sabom, was highly skeptical of Moody's findings. However...

- Over a five year period he interviewed and compiled data on 116 persons who had had a close brush with death. Of these, 71 reported one form or another of near-death experience...Sabom conducted extended interviews with the ten who had detailed recollections, either of resuscitations or surgery. The results were astonishing. In every case, the accounts jibed with standard medical procedures; moreover, where medical records were available, the records of the procedures and the accounts of the patients perfectly matched. In all of these cases, [unconscious] patients observed details that they could not possibly have observed from their physical vantage point.[3]

Journalist and former atheist, Lee Strobel, adds:

- In their journal article, Sam Parnia and Peter Fenwick, a neuropsychiatrist at the Institute of Psychiatry in London, describe their study of sixty-three heart attack victims who were declared clinically dead but were later revived and interviewed. About ten percent reported having well-structured, lucid thought processes, with memory formation and reasoning, during the time that their brains were not functioning. The effects of oxygen starvation or drugs—objections commonly offered by skeptics—were ruled out as factors.[4]

This contradicts the atheist narrative that thinking and choosing depend *exclusively* upon physical brain activity. In order to maintain this narrow materialistic worldview, atheists are forced to discount these kinds of studies, along with the numerous accounts of extra-body experiences.

In another study, it was found that consciousness—and consequently, free will—can exist apart from a functioning brain:

- Of the 2,060 patients from Austria, the US and the UK interviewed for the study who had survived cardiac arrest, almost 40 per cent said that they recall some form of awareness after being pronounced clinically dead.

- Of those who said they had experienced some awareness, just two per cent said their experience was consistent with the feeling of an outer body experience—where one feels completely aware and can hear and see what's going on around them after death. Almost half of the respondents said the experience was not of awareness, but rather of fear.[5]

One man was able to recall what had happened in the hospital with "eerie accuracy" after he had died temporarily.

Findings from near-death experiences like these and the following have often been reported:

- The detailed recollections of visual awareness in this case were consistent with verified events.[6]

This is significant, since it has often been assumed that experiences in relation to death are likely hallucinations or illusions.

So then, why are these kinds of findings so often ignored? Simply put, *they do not fit the prevailing materialistic paradigm that nothing exists outside of the physical world*. To suggest otherwise opens the door to considerations about the existence of God—a rather inconvenient truth.

THE COSTS OF DENYING FREE WILL AND CULPABILITY

DFC is humanly demeaning.

This is significant because our understanding of free will and our culpability has a major effect on how we view ourselves, those around us, and how we treat them. If we view human beings as no more than sophisticated chemical machines, it is more likely that we will use them like machines. Furthermore, if one takes this philosophy to its logical conclusion, then people would likely be destroyed when they no longer serve any utilitarian purpose.

DFC undermines everything upon which civilization is based—justice, our understanding of right and wrong, and how we view reward and punishment.

A world where we cannot do other than what we have been pre-determined to do has no room for a genuine appreciation for the concepts of virtue or justice. If it was biology *alone* that made the rapist rape, then how could it be just to punish him? After all, there is no way that he could have made any other choice. As a consequence, how could any punishment be just? Conversely, in such a world, how could any reward for exemplary behavior be considered as deserving? All of these issues would be merely a matter of chemistry. Morality or justice would have nothing to do with any of it.

Chapter 5

DFC is a major threat
even to the very existence and well-being of civilization.

Those who deny free will and our culpability nevertheless acknowledge the need for punishment. But their conception of punishment does not rely on any appreciation for truth or justice. Instead of an objective standard for that which is right, it becomes only a matter of "might makes right." And what "might" would that be? The might of the majority to protect their own interests.

Yes, a society based on these underpinnings would bring charges against a burglar. But he would be charged, not because he deserves punishment, but because he has violated the interests of the majority. There can be no real justice when people believe that "justice" is merely a made-up concept.

What will the denier of free will teach his son? What will school systems in such a world teach their students? Would a teacher actually tell an unruly student that he or she could not have acted otherwise because there is no right and wrong? In such an absurd scenario, the student would have every right to ask, "Why then am I being punished?" If the student is then lectured about how he has violated the norms of society and must be restrained from doing so, the teacher will surely be planting destructive seeds of cynicism and contempt...or a slavish conformism. No civilization can survive on such a shoddy foundation.

DFC is the death of honesty
and all meaningful relationships.

When someone who denies free will and culpability is caught having an affair, he could honestly say, "I could not have acted otherwise, so don't blame me." Instead, resolving interpersonal conflicts like this requires much more from an offender. "Please forgive me. I know I really hurt you terribly. I promise never to do this again!" However, biochemical machines cannot truthfully make such promises. They are quite limited in how they can react. The following pledge would be much more likely: "If my biochemistry permits, I will not do this again." But this would scarcely be an adequate response. Consequently, the worldview of one who denies free will forces her to live a life characterized by irresponsibility and dishonesty.

DFC undermines our motivation.

If we are hard-wired to do only what our biochemistry determines, why bother trying our hand at anything?

DFC logically undermines itself.

How? Those who deny free will and culpability believe that their thinking has been entirely determined by biochemical reactions. Therefore, how could such people believe in anything apart from what their biochemistry had already determined? Going one step further, if our thinking is entirely pre-determined, it leaves little room for considering the truth of any idea, even the "truth" of DFC.

❖ ❖ ❖

Why do intelligent people become DFCs?

Why do we confine ourselves in narrow, dysfunctional boxes which constrict the way we view ourselves and all of life? What is the payoff for denying free will? One friend explained the great relief he experienced once he had rejected free will. He felt that he was no longer responsible for his behavior; his sense of guilt was diminished. He no longer had to blame himself for not living up to his moral ideals.

Who can lay any blame at this man's feet for living this way? His wife can! Especially when she unleashes a barrage of blame on him when she catches him cheating on her. And his lame rebuttal—"I couldn't do otherwise"—is guaranteed to mean absolutely nothing to her. What if he were to apologize? But why would or should he apologize if he was powerless in his circumstances to behave in any other way? This way of living simply does not work in the real world. Furthermore, when we play these mind-games with ourselves, we are in effect diminishing our humanity.

How then do we deal with our crippling feelings of guilt and shame without minimizing our culpability?

It doesn't seem that we can meaningfully forgive ourselves. Self-forgiveness is no more than psychological masturbation, while true forgiveness is necessarily relational. If my wife accuses me of cheating on her, it would not help to bring about reconciliation if I were to merely say, "Well, I have forgiven myself." Instead, we need the assurances that Christ Himself has forgiven us and has removed our sins and moral failures. It is only with this assurance that we can take full responsibility for our transgressions. This is the kind of mind-set and manner of life that enables us to live coherently.

In contrast, when deniers of free will realize that they can't actually live that way, their "gurus" offer up an astonishing solution for their dilemma: People should just live *as if they have free will!* However, this nonsensical inconsistency should lead them to consider a paradigm more in line with the facts of our existence, rather than playing make-believe.

How does our free will provide evidence for God's existence?

The concept of free will and the exercise of it in our daily lives suggests that there is another world beyond the material world, a spiritual world of which we may partake. As one atheist put it:

- "If our mind is purely material, then each atom and molecule is totally governed— pre-determined—by the laws of science. This eliminates any possibility of human autonomy or self-determination."

Free will strongly suggests that our minds are more than just a repository for matter. Instead, there seems to be a reality that lies beyond the material realm—the spirit. If the spirit exists, then its source must be an uncreated Creator of spirits. And if this indeed is the truth, then the naturalistic/materialistic worldview can be assigned to its well-deserved grave.

The next chapters will expand on this theme.

CAN IRRATIONALITY PRODUCE RATIONALITY?

CHAPTER SUMMARY
Free will is essential for any explanation of rationality. Free will also points strongly to ID—Intelligent Design—and to a non-material reality.

Atheistic, naturalistic evolution assumes that non-life produced life. Among many other things, this means that mindless natural selection is the sole architect of the amazing, astounding, thinking mind, with its billions of neurons and its trillions of neuronal connections.

Atheist-turned-Christian C.S. Lewis doubted that this was possible. He compared mindless evolution to someone with a damaged brain:

- Whenever you know what the other man is saying is wholly due to his complexes or to a bit of bone pressing on his brain, you cease to attach importance to it. But if naturalism were true then all thoughts whatever would be wholly the result of irrational causes. Therefore, all thoughts would be completely worthless. Therefore, naturalism is completely worthless. If this is true, then we can know no truths. It cuts its own throat.[1]

Although I sympathize with Lewis' reasoning, I think that it would leave most naturalists undaunted, unaffected. After all, such people already believe that our eyes are fully capable of producing a perfect facsimile or image of the physical world, in actual time, by means of strictly mindless processes. If biochemical machinations can produce our vision, why could they not also enable us to think?

However, our thinking seems to transcend even what our eyes are able to do. While our eyes can see, possibly because of deterministic and invariable laws of biochemistry which do not

50

require free will, it would be much harder to accept that our thinking came about in the same way.

Our thinking capacities would need to be of a very rudimentary nature if they were to be entirely determined by unvarying biochemical forces. If this were so, it would mean that our thinking would, of necessity, be determined by laws locked into predictable and formulaic patterns.

However, this is precisely what human thought is not! For our thinking to discover truth, it needs the freedom and flexibility that deterministic laws do not allow. Deterministic forces mechanically reproduce the same patterns. That is precisely what makes them predictable. Conversely, true thinking and discovery has to be able to take wings and fly above social, biological, and psychological bonds.

I had this experience as I began to grow in Christ. As a new Christian, I had the perplexing realization that there were thoughts that I wanted to think, ideas that I wanted to mentally pursue—and yet I was unable to think them. There were places I wanted to take my mind, but my mind refused to take me there. Looking back, I can see now that I was locked into the rut of my own thinking.

Over the years, as I have continued to use my mind, I have experienced a greater freedom to focus, to explore and to discover. I have found that I have been able to ask questions of myself and then find the answers. It seems to me that this is the same freedom an artist experiences as he or she creates. Amazingly, the more we use our minds, the more they seem to expand.

If all thinking is pre-determined by predictable, formulaic forces, it would have been impossible for me to realize, in such a tangible way, my liberation from the mental prison which had held me captive.

Chapter 6

A LOGICAL RESTATEMENT

Since a logical restatement can provide clarity, let me try to restate what I have been saying in a logical form:

> PREMISE #1: Thinking and creativity require freedom of thought.
>
> PREMISE #2: Materialism, naturalism, and deterministic biochemical causation provide no basis for freedom of thought. Instead, such deterministic forces only produce repeating, predictable patterns.
>
> CONCLUSION: Freedom of thought must transcend mere materialistic/naturalistic causation.

PREMISE #1: Thinking and creativity require freedom of thought.

We all experience freedom of thought and choice. To doubt this is like doubting our most basic perceptions, like doubting our personhood or our experiences. For example, I would think it absurd if someone told me, at this moment in time, that I am not sitting in front of my computer. Likewise, it is equally absurd to deny that we possess and experience the freedom of thought and choice.

Here is what Tolstoy had to say about this in *War and Peace:*

- "You say: I am not free. But I have raised and lowered my arm. Everyone understands that this illogical answer is an irrefutable proof of freedom."[2]

We all know, innately, that we have the capacity to focus our minds to solve problems. Furthermore, we know that we are not locked into a pre-determined and formulaic biochemical pattern of thinking to solve those problems. Admittedly, we must confess that there are occasions when we find ourselves locked into a mental rut where we are obsessing repeatedly about certain thoughts. However, these experiences should serve to highlight those other occasions when we are thinking clearly. If all our thoughts are entirely biochemically predetermined, how would we be able to differentiate between these very different states of mind? The simple fact of the matter is that we couldn't.

Are we being deluded? Hardly! The way some see these issues, though, we should even question whether the car coming towards us might actually be a bicycle or even an airplane. But if we question such direct perceptions, then maybe we should also question all of our perceptions. Do we even exist? Maybe we are merely the internal machinations of a computer or only a tiny segment of some sort of universal consciousness. Perhaps all of the evidence that we can marshal in favor of rational thought and even our existence is also illusory.

Instead, it seems to me that it is more logical to accept our perceptions. Furthermore, it seems more evidentially consistent to question the radical skepticism of naturalistic thinking and acknowledge that, to some varying extent, we are indeed able to direct our thoughts.

When I ride my bicycle, my senses of sight and hearing serve me admirably. If I try to text while riding, I cannot see or hear as well, and thus the likelihood of an accident increases dramatically. This illustration about my senses also applies to rational thinking. When I do not make use of the full range of my thought processes, it is much more likely that I will make foolish and costly decisions.

PREMISE #2: Materialism, naturalism, and deterministic biochemical causation provide no basis for freedom of thought. Instead, such deterministic forces only produce repeating, predictable patterns.

Atheists tend to agree that materialism eliminates any basis for free will, or our freedom of thought. In *Consciousness Explained*, atheist and materialist, Daniel C. Dennett, acknowledged that materialists deny free will:

- But recently I have learned from discussions with a variety of scientists and other non-philosophers (e.g., the scientists participating with me in the Sean Carroll workshop on the future of naturalism) that they lean the other way: free will, in their view, is obviously incompatible with naturalism, with determinism, and very likely incoherent against any background, so they cheerfully insist that of course they don't have free will, couldn't have free will, but so what? It has nothing to do with morality or the meaning of life. Their advice to me at the symposium was simple: recast my pressing question as to whether naturalism (materialism, determinism, science...) has any implications for what we may call moral competence. For instance, does neuroscience show that we cannot be responsible for our choices, cannot justifiably be praised or blamed, rewarded or punished? Abandon the term 'free will' to the libertarians and other incompatibilists, who can pursue their fantasies untroubled. Note that this is not a dismissal of the important issues; it's a proposal about which camp gets to use, and define, the term. I am beginning to appreciate the benefits of discarding the term 'free will' altogether, but that course too involves a lot of heavy lifting, if one is to avoid being misunderstood.[3]

Another atheist and free will denier is Sam Harris. In *Free Will*, Harris wrote:

- You can do what you decide to do—but you cannot decide what you will decide to do.[4]

In other words, we humans are not free to decide or even to direct our thoughts and creative expressions. However, many of the same people who deny free will and freedom of thought counsel us to live our lives *as if we were free, as if our lives have meaning, and even as if there were objective moral truths.* In other words, our optimal survival strategy is to live a life of make-believe!

Those who have worked hardest to dethrone God in the name of rationality, liberty, and the alleged vindictiveness of God have concluded that the best life is to be pursued by denying the following: the very existence of reason and freedom, objective moral truths, and intellectual integrity. How could we not minimize and diminish the very substance of our lives and the lives of others if we decide to live in such a manner, even to the denying of our own senses? Should we not, instead, adopt a theory of life based upon the actual, verifiable facts of life?

CONCLUSION:
Freedom of thought must transcend mere materialistic/naturalistic causation.

The activity of the mind seems to transcend the deterministic laws of science.

The cause must always be greater than the effect. If the effect is greater, it would mean that some aspect of the effect is uncaused. This also excludes the possibility of self-causation. A rational, free mind is greater than any natural, mindless cause. Therefore, what is non-rational cannot produce what is far greater—a rational and free mind.

In declaring that we are created in the image of God, the Bible claims that we are more than just material objects—wet machines—as some call us. We are endowed with a transcendent dignity and freedom.

❖ ❖ ❖

One final point: When we deny our God-given dignity, we demean ourselves and the rest of humanity. We relegate ourselves to the status of animals, albeit functionally sophisticated ones. However, this comes with great cost. Psychologist James Hillman understandably insists that we need to reclaim our true identity from the deadening, materialistic ways in which we usually interpret our lives:

- We dull our lives by the way we conceive them…By accepting the idea that I am the effect of…hereditary and social forces, I reduce myself to a result. The more my life is accounted for by what already occurred in my chromosomes, by what my parents did or didn't do, and by my early years now long past, the more my biography is the story of a victim. I am living a plot written by my genetic code, ancestral heredity, traumatic occasions, parental unconsciousness, societal accidents.[5]

When we reject God, we also reject ourselves and the dignity He has given us. In the process, we also reject others and their inherent value. The Bible does not support such a flawed perspective. After the flood, God cautioned Noah:

- "And for your lifeblood I will require a reckoning: from every beast I will require it and from man. From his fellow man I will require a reckoning for the life of man. 'Whoever sheds the blood of man, by man shall his blood be shed, for God made man in his own image.'" (Genesis 9:5-6, invoking Genesis 1:26-27)

When we reject our divine origin, we also reject it in other people. This can give us the unauthorized license to treat others with less dignity than they deserve. They, in turn, can treat us and everyone we love in the same manner. This might not be apparent to us now, but as clouds must precede rain, so too a diminished view of humanity will eventually bring about the debased treatment of multitudes. We must not forget the abominations of godless Nazism and Communism.

When we apply the Creator's insight about our origins to the people around us, we will be more inclined to treat them as the wonderfully-created beings that they are. Conversely—and sadly—people who reject God and embrace atheistic materialism have no reasonable or defensible grounds upon which they may value themselves…or anyone else.

EVIDENCE THAT CONSCIOUSNESS DOES NOT REQUIRE A LIVING, PHYSICAL BODY

CHAPTER SUMMARY

What if consciousness exists apart from our physical bodies? If this is so, it would signify that there is a dimension of existence that affirms the Biblical worldview, lying beyond the grasp of naturalistic explanation. Furthermore, if this is so, then many would need to revise their worldview. They would have to acknowledge the reality of the world of spirits and surrender the worldview that they had held—their belief in naturalism, materialism, and perhaps even atheism. Instead, people who espouse these various philosophies have taken an easier path. They simply proclaim—dogmatically— that science is the only measure of truth, which is scientism; and, that spiritual realities are not within the purview of science.

However, it seems that even science has something to say about the idea of disembodied consciousness. As we have already noted in the discussion about free will and culpability in Chapter 5, here are the findings of one study:

- Of the 2,060 patients from Austria, the US and the UK interviewed for the study who had survived cardiac arrest, almost 40 per cent said that they recall some form of awareness after being pronounced clinically dead.[1]

These kinds of findings are not unusual. *Wikipedia* mentions a few more studies:

- In a review article B. Greyson refers to van Lommel's study (as well as other sources) and mentions that there have been "documented and corroborated accurate perceptions by near-death experiencers of incidents that occurred during the time when the brain was fully anesthetized or deprived of blood flow, as during cardiac arrest or respiratory arrest." B. Greyson also mentions that apparently some patients reported events that occurred beyond what their sense organs could perceive and that would have been impossible for them to perceive even in a conscious state.[2]

- Another review article reports that 41 (12%) of the cardiac arrest patients interviewed provided accounts similar to the Sam Parnia's 2001(*sic*) study...One patient had a conventional out of body experience where he reported being able to watch and recall events during the time of his cardiac arrest. His claims were confirmed by hospital personnel. "This did not appear consistent with hallucinatory or illusory experiences, as the recollections were compatible with real and verifiable rather than imagined events."[3]

These findings point powerfully to another reality, a spiritual reality, beyond the physical realm. If this is so, then the existence of a supreme Spirit Being from which all other spiritual entities derive their existence, becomes very probable.

P. van Lommel concluded:

- How could a clear consciousness outside one's body be experienced at the moment that the brain no longer functions during a period of clinical death with flat EEG?... (the) NDE [near death experience/near death experiencer] pushes at the limits of medical ideas about the range of human consciousness and the mind-brain relation.[4]

Cardiologist Michael Sabom had been highly skeptical. However, after conducting extensive interviews with 71 NDEs, he concluded that:

- In all of these cases, [NDE] patients observed details that they could not possibly have observed from their physical vantage point.[5]

Due to reported out-of-body-experiences, some of the subjects in various studies were even able to report what was transpiring in the next room. In another curious analysis, Kenneth Ring, Professor Emeritus of Psychology at the University of Connecticut, and Sharon Cooper, conducted a two-year study into the NDEs of the blind. They published their findings in a 1999 book, *Mindsight*, where...

- ...they documented the solid evidence of 31 cases in which blind people report visually accurate information obtained during an NDE. Perhaps the best example in his study is that of a forty-five-year-old blind woman by the name of Vicki Umipeg. Vicki was born blind; her optic nerve having been completely destroyed at birth because of an excess of oxygen she received in the incubator. Yet, she appears to have been able to see during her NDE. Her story is a particularly clear instance of how NDEs of the congenitally blind can unfold in precisely the same way as do those of sighted persons.[6]

If even some of these many accounts can be trusted, they argue very persuasively for an extra-material consciousness.

However, such findings are routinely ignored. Case studies like the ones I have mentioned do not fit the prevailing materialistic paradigm claiming that nothing exists outside of the physical world. To suggest otherwise opens the door to considerations about the existence of God—an inconvenient and uncomfortable truth. Some evolutionists have gone so far as to admit that God must be resisted at all costs:

- We take the side of science in spite of the patent absurdity of some of its constructs...in spite of the tolerance of the scientific community for unsubstantiated commitment to materialism...we are forced by our a *priori* adherence to material causes to create an apparatus of investigation and set of concepts that produce material explanations, no matter how counterintuitive, no matter how mystifying to the uninitiated. Moreover, that materialism is absolute, for we cannot allow a Divine Foot in the door.[7]

- Even if all the data point to an intelligent designer, such a hypothesis is excluded from science because it is not naturalistic.[8]

Nevertheless, it cannot be denied that scientific exploration of the physical world has provided evidence for the spiritual world. Interestingly, the founders of modern neuroscience were actually dualists. They believed that the physical brain could connect with that which is non-physical, similar to the way a TV can make a connection with electromagnetic waves. Today, there are precious few professionals in the sciences who wish to be associated with dualism:

- Dualism reigned unchallenged in Western thought until recent times, and the founders of modern neuroscience, Charles Sherrington, Wilder Penfield, and John Eccles, were all dualists.[9]

One of these doctors, Wilder Penfield, freely admitted that he had patients whose responses seemed to be extra-physical:

- Penfield would stimulate electrically the proper motor cortex of the conscious patients and challenge them to keep one hand from moving when the current was applied. The patient would seize this hand with the other hand and struggle to hold it still. Thus, one hand under the control of the electrical current and the other hand under the control of the patient's mind fought against each other. Penfield risked the explanation that the patient had not only a physical brain that was stimulated to action but also a nonphysical reality that interacted with the brain.[10]

Penfield found that his patients could distinguish between responses that had been electrically stimulated from those that were self-stimulated. This would suggest that some actions, decisions, and beliefs lie beyond the strictly physical:

- Invariably the patient would respond, by saying, "I didn't do that; you did..." No matter how much Penfield probed the cerebral cortex, he said, "There is no place...where electrical stimulation will cause a patient to believe or to decide." That's because those functions originate in the conscious self, not the brain. A lot of subsequent research has validated this. When Roger Sperry and his team studied the differences between the brain's right and left hemispheres, they discovered the mind has a causal power independent of the brain's activities. This led Sperry to conclude [that] materialism was false.[11]

If the brain is entirely a physical entity, then we should expect that every type of mental activity could be stimulated electrically. But this is not the case. Scientific findings like these affirm that our choices are not totally determined by chemical-electrical responses. In fact, the very notion of free will contradicts materialism.

The free will problem is daunting for the materialist. If everything is biochemically determined, there is no room for free will or anything that is self-initiated. Once materialists deny the existence of anything outside the physical world, they also deny any possibility of free will. Many materialists choose to dismiss the existence of free will entirely.

Adherence to the tenets of materialism comes at a prohibitively high price. This worldview denies many of the values that materialists would like to exalt, like human equality. Yet, how can there be such a thing as human equality if materialists only recognize human worth in terms of education, sex, strength, appearance, and contributions to society? According to these criteria, some people represent a cost to society while others represent a contribution. As a result, materialists have no basis upon which to believe that there exists such a thing as human equality! They can only make believe that it exists because it is a useful construct, helping to ensure the smooth running of society.

Chapter 7

THE "SPIRIT" WORLD

There are also other reasons to believe that an extra-material world exists. For example, I know beyond a shadow of a doubt that there are lying spirits, or demons. This firsthand knowledge is important, especially for someone like me, a skeptic by nature and thoroughly imbued with the Western prejudice against the world of spirits.

I have two cousins who used to "play" with a Ouija Board when they were 10 and 12. It terrified them, but we adults pressured them to bring it out at a family event. The results were nothing short of amazing. When the girls placed their four hands upon it, the disc literally raced around the board. It spelled out words as fast as we could record them. The words became sentences and then thoughts and stories, communicating things that the girls would have been incapable of knowing, things that should have been beyond their ability to express.

Our hyper-skeptical family then blindfolded the girls. This did not impede their performance in the slightest. Even today, my atheistic family has no natural explanation for what we experienced.

I was so impressed with what I had seen that I persuaded my girlfriend to try the Ouija with me. I remember clearly that the spirits we conjured were very liberal in their use of profanity. Beyond that, they answered all our questions. I had naively thought that they could be trusted, assuming that they were ascended spirits, enlightened beings who had evolved past any interest in lying. Then we asked them the big question: "Is there a God?" To this, they answered, "Ouija!"

At around this same time, my parents' home was burglarized. We asked the spirits to disclose the identity of the perpetrators. They seemed eager to identify the neighbors of my parents. Immediately, I decided that I would take revenge upon them. Fortunately for all concerned, the police apprehended the real perpetrators before I could take action.

Since then, through my study of the Scriptures, I have come to understand that these spirit beings are evil, which I should have realized years before:

- …for Satan himself masquerades as an angel of light. It is not surprising, then, if his servants masquerade as servants of righteousness. Their end will be what their actions deserve. (2 Corinthians 11:14-15)

Recently, a student told me of her own experiences with the world of spirits:

- As a teenager I often hung out with large groups of people of various ages, some my age and some adults and little children. One week during the winter, we decided to perform séances for 3 nights. Incidents did occur, but for the first 2 days I was stuck babysitting the little ones, so I couldn't see what was happening. I was usually told the next day by someone in the group or by a boyfriend of mine at the time. He would tell me that he couldn't remember everything because as soon as the praying or chanting started, he would fall asleep. When it was over, he would wake up to find that the cross hanging around his neck would be broken and on his lap. When the séances were on, although I was in a closed room, I could still hear a lot of commotion going on and even some screams. I just had to be at one of these things to see what was going on. So, on the last night of the séances, I decided to speak up and say that I didn't want to take care of the kids that night. I sat with my boyfriend and the chanting/praying started. We were all in a circle, sitting around the room. I don't remember if we held hands or not. The person who was the medium was the same for all the nights of the séances. It was a woman and she would sit at the head of the circle in a chair and start the chanting while we all listened. Right away my boyfriend fell asleep and I knew something was going to happen. I looked at the woman and her face seemed darker, so I left my chair and approached her out of curiosity. Why was it I could see her body, but close to her head it looked like a dark shadow was there. When I came close, I noticed her eyes seemed to be crooked; they were looking straight ahead as if she didn't know I was there. I called her name and she didn't answer. Someone from the group told me to stay seated. They proceeded to talk to this woman, but the voice that came out of her was a man's voice and very deep. I was a little scared and tried to wake up my boyfriend. He wouldn't wake up, so I just sat down next to him again. All of a sudden out of nowhere, the woman started screaming and ran toward the kitchen. Some of the men, including her husband, ran after her to try to calm her down. That deep voice kept saying that he had to throw her out of the window. Finally, after she was pulled to the floor and restrained, one of the other people started praying over her. After that I decided not to partake in any of those things again. It was too scary.

I have found that incidents like this have been experienced by many others. Relief was found only by calling upon Jesus.

Years ago, after I had been convinced of the reality of evil spirits, I felt as if there must be some other spirits who could be viewed as "good." I learned that a man named Jungleman, a Yanomamo shaman-turned-Christian, had also been convinced that the spirits he was experiencing were divine, god-like beings. However, in *Spirit of the Rainforest*, he finally confessed:

- I wish I had known the truth about [Jesus] when I was a young man—it would have saved me so much pain and misery. But how could I? My spirits lied so much to me and tricked me. They were so beautiful, so wonderful, so hard not to want. They were the best at telling me split-truth. Now I'm at the end of this life, and I'm ready to begin my real life with [Jesus].[12]

THE HIGH PRICE-TAG OF SPIRITISM

In *The Facts on Spirit Guides*, John Ankerberg and John Weldon sound the alarm about this often-ignored world. They warn of the strong association between spiritism and mental illness:

- One discovers many mental patients who are mentally ill precisely because they are demonized. This is born out by the research of German psychiatrist and parapsychologist Hans Bender who coined the term "mediumistic psychosis"; by theologian and psychologist Kurt Koch; and by clinical psychologist and Swedenborgian Wilson Van Dusen, who has examined thousands of patients and noted the parallels to spiritistic experiences and phenomena.[13]

However, the spirits are too shrewd to advertise the costs of dabbling in this realm. One of those costs is suicide. According to Ankerberg and Weldon, there have been...

- ...innumerable cases where the 'loving' spirits have deliberately induced emotional dependence upon their advice and then at a moment of weakness encouraged their contact to commit suicide. And this has been occurring for decades, probably even centuries. In the 1920 text *The Menace of Spiritualism*, case after case of tragedy is listed.[14]

The same authors have compiled their own list of additional horrors that have stalked those who have become involved in the occult:

- Arthur Ford became a morphine addict and alcoholic...Bishop Pike died a tragic death...The biography on [Edgar] Cayce by Joseph Millar reveals the extent of suffering Cayce's occultic involvement cost him—from psychic attacks to mysterious fires...Many channelers seem to succumb to various vices later in life.[15]

Although Ankerberg and Weldon describe the medium M. Lamar Keene as "fraudulent," they felt that his words were instructive, so they quote them in their book:

- 'All the mediums I've known or known about have had tragic endings. The Fox sisters, who started it all, wound up as alcoholic derelicts. William Slade...died insane in a Michigan sanitarium. Margery, the medium, lay on her deathbed a hopeless drunk...Wherever I looked it was the same: mediums, at the end of their tawdry life, dying a tawdry death.'[16]

Violence was another price to be paid:

- Spiritist and guru Sri Chinmoy, a spiritual advisor at the United Nations observes, 'Many, many black magicians and people who deal with spirits have been strangled or killed. I know because I've been near quite a few of these cases.'[17]

- Dr. Kurt Koch observed after 45 years of counseling the occultly oppressed that from his own experience 'numerous cases of suicide, fatal accidents, strokes and insanity are to be observed among occult practitioners...Anyone who has had to observe for 45 years the effects of spiritism can only warn people with all the strength at his disposal.'[18]

These observations parallel the global research regarding the fate of spiritistic cultures. In *Whence the "Noble Savage,"* Patrick Frank summarized the research regarding the analysis of ancient burial sites of spiritistic cultures. His findings demonstrate that the violent death rates of British Columbian Native Americans—27-33%—far exceeded even the violent death rate of 20th century Europe and the US, which stands at 1%. Frank also adds:

- The Southwest [of the U.S.] is dotted with finds of people killed en masse...These indications of war, violent deaths, mutilations and cannibalism are from tribal societies that experienced no European or modern contact, thus contradicting the idea that peoples who were free from European influence lived relatively peaceful lives.[19]

Spiritistic societies build no hospitals; nor do they establish any universities or any other enduring institutions. Instead, according to their own reports, they have been spirit-ravaged. Ankerberg and Weldon have listed several books by spiritists who have found refuge in Christ:

1. *I Talked with Spirits,* by Victor Ernest
2. *Out from Darkness,* by Ben Alexander
3. *The Challenging Counterfeit,* by Raphel Gasson

Here is what these partners in research—Ankerberg and Welden—have concluded:

- What is amazing is that the evidence is there for all to see and yet it is ignored.[20]

❖ ❖ ❖

What does all of this say about the existence of God? For one thing, it demonstrates that consciousness does not require a physical body. Neither does God.

In addition, it suggests that the existence of evil spirits also requires the existence of a spiritual Being—God—that is good. Why would I say this? For the most part, the condition of our world and our lives is just too comfortable for evil to be in absolute control. We live in a world of order, for the most part. This has enabled us to gain some mastery over our lives. In addition, the needs we have are largely satisfied. We hunger, and there is food; we thirst, and there is water; we tire, and there is sleep; we feel lonely, and there are friends and family.

This would suggest that there must be a higher and more benign Spirit to account for our benign condition, as the Apostle Paul had reasoned with the pagan spiritists:

- Yet he [God] did not leave himself without witness [the evidence of His goodness], for he did good by giving you rains from heaven and fruitful seasons, satisfying your hearts with food and gladness. (Acts 14:17)

For the most part, this has proven to be a world of some pleasure and fulfillment, at least in part. Conversely, this is not the world that we would expect if it had been exclusively the creation of demons.

This often raises an additional and related question: How do we know that there isn't a pantheon of creator gods, or spirits?

Polytheism is problematic for a number of reasons:

1. Many gods require many additional leaps of faith to explain the origin of each one of them, making polytheism even more improbable.

2. Many gods mean many conflicting opinions. However, this world is knowable and predictable. This calls for the existence of one omnipotent and all-wise Being holding everything together and insuring the harmonious and integrated operation of the cosmos.

3. The laws of science are elegant and immutable. This tends to rule against the idea of a collection of competing gods, all with their hands on the wheel.

THE FINE-TUNING OF THE UNIVERSE AND THE VAIN ATTEMPT TO AVOID GOD WITH THE MULTIVERSE

CHAPTER SUMMARY

The incredible fine-tuning of the universe points to a Designer. Consequently, the naturalist/materialist must come up with an alternative explanation—an infinite number of universes. If there is an infinite number, then the laws of chance would argue that one of them would be ours. One problem: there is absolutely no evidence for even a second universe.

- Aristotle believed in "...an intelligent natural world that functions according to some deliberate design."[1]

- Albert Einstein believed that..."The most incomprehensible thing about the universe is that it is comprehensible."[2]

Both of these statements, by men living several thousand years apart, are plausible because of the truth of the observation of the late physicist Stephen Hawking:

- Everything in the universe follows laws, without exception.[3]

It is because of these laws that we are enabled to "do" science and even to predict future events on the basis of them.

Hawking adds that even the characteristics of the entire universe "...appear to have a design that is both tailor–made to support us and, if we are to exist, leaves little room for alteration." This means that all of the physical constants—whether they be gravitational, or nuclear, or any of at least 30 other forces—have been precisely calibrated to support existence, even life. Consequently, none of these forces can be altered without serious consequences. We call this the "fine-tuning of the universe." And, as it turns out, this fine-tuning has been meticulously engineered for us and for our well-being.

This seems to be an indisputable fact. According to British astrophysicist George Ellis:

- Amazing fine tuning occurs in the laws that make this [complexity] possible. Realization of the complexity of what is accomplished makes it very difficult not to use the word 'miraculous' without taking a stand as to the ontological status of the word.[4]

Cambridge micro-physicist Sir John Polkinghorne came to the same conclusion:

- When you realize that the laws of nature must be incredibly finely tuned to produce the universe we see, that conspires to plant the idea that the universe did not just happen, but that there must be a purpose behind it.[5]

To what can we liken this? Imagine entering a restaurant and finding dozens of "Happy Birthday" balloons floating in the air with your name painted on each one. Your favorite foods are beautifully laid out on a table, and all of your friends are gathered together. Everything has been carefully designed to celebrate your birthday. You know it instantly—someone had planned it for you.

Yet, this is the very conclusion that materialistic secularists are desperate to avoid. They will do anything to keep any sort of a notion of God from getting His foot in the door. Consequently, in his latest book, Hawking writes:

- The discovery recently of so many laws of nature could lead some back to the idea that this grand design is the work of a grand Designer. Yet the latest advances in cosmology explain why the laws of the universe seem tailor-made for humans, without the need for a benevolent creator.[6]

How do these "advances in cosmology" shed light upon the universe? By some calculations, in order for our fine-tuned universe to appear naturally, the odds would be...one chance out of 10 followed by a hundred zeros—a figure which is more than the number of atoms in the entire universe. However, to counter the seeming impossibility of such an unlikely, improbable estimate, Hawking rather glibly offered:

- As recent advances in cosmology suggest, the laws of gravity and quantum theory allow universes to appear spontaneously from nothing.[7]

This is not science at all, but only wishful thinking! There is not the smallest speck of hard, observable evidence that there is even one separate universe, let alone an uncountable number, as Hawking's theory would require. He surmises that if there is such a number of universes, then it would stand to reason that one of them would be just right for us. Thus, life as we know it would—once again—magically appear.

But this view would reduce all of life to a cheap game of chance. If you throw ten dice a countless number of times, ten "sixes" are bound to come up at least once. However, life is infinitely more complex than throwing dice.

If we think a little further about what Hawking is saying, we might also be asking ourselves: "How can Hawking appeal to the laws of gravity and quantum theory to justify his highly imaginative idea that multiple universes could spring into existence?"

For one thing, there are no "laws of gravity and quantum theory" in nothingness, unless they always existed. Yet, if we are going to consider eternal, uncaused causes of everything, should we not consider an adequate *single* cause before all else? After all, the laws of scientific inquiry cannot account for the existence of time, space, or matter, let alone a single pebble. They only act upon pre-existing objects. Therefore, how could another universe spring into existence...from nothing? Hawking's theory has no adequate answer for this.

In the face of these problems, Hawking insists on a "spontaneous creation":

- Spontaneous creation is the reason there is something rather than nothing, why the universe exists, why we exist. It is not necessary to invoke God.[8]

Hawking is fighting a losing battle against God. The idea of "spontaneous generation" was rejected years ago, and with good reason. I am sure that many of us wish that a few thousand dollars would just spontaneously appear in the palm of our hand, but that just doesn't seem to happen. Nor does such a thing occur in the world of science. Instead, science is founded on the presupposition that everything that begins to exist—or change—has a cause.

At this point in our discussion, an evolutionist might make this charge:

- "This is just another God-in-the-gaps argument. You assume that there must be a God to explain existence because science has yet to provide any convincing rationale for one. However, it is only a matter of time until science provides that explanation."

There are several critical assumptions buried beneath the surface here:

1. **Science can explain everything.** The fact that science has provided many explanations does not mean that science can provide *all* explanations. In fact, science has provided absolutely no evidence for anyone to assume that "science can explain everything."

2. **Scientific explanations supplant God.** Not so. Scientific explanations affirm the presence of God and of His exquisite design on every level.

3. **Scientific explanations support an anti-God hypothesis—God vs. Science.** Instead, scientific

explanations call into question the idea that things just happen, or that they simply "appear." Science is founded upon a foundation of elegant, immutable, and universal laws—all of which bear the unmistakable imprint of the Transcendent.

Science has also demonstrated that all systems eventually break down. This is in direct opposition to the naturalistic presupposition that systems grow in functionality and information. Isn't it interesting that entropy, the 2nd Law of Thermodynamics—the idea that everything has a tendency to break down—was anticipated by creationism?

4. **The basis of science is naturalism.** There is no evidence that science requires naturalistic assumptions. In fact, there is no scientific evidence that anything has ever been caused naturalistically, without design. Yet, most scientists continue to support naturalism and reject intelligent design.

Returning once again to my birthday illustration, birthday parties do not magically appear. They are planned and engineered by agents—in most cases, family and friends—who have adequate intelligence and resources to make them happen. If Hawking had claimed that his multiple universes were caused by a turtle, for example, he would be ridiculed and scorned by the university community. However, he is asserting something even more absurd—that the universe was caused by a "causer" less than a turtle. He wants us to believe that the universe came into being from nothing at all! I'll put my money on the turtle. Better yet, I'll invest it in an omnipotent God who has proven Himself in so many ways.

I am not alone in rejecting the multiverse hypothesis. In *Discover Magazine*, Tim Folger, expressed similar doubts:

• Short of invoking a benevolent creator, many physicists see only one possible explanation: Our universe may be but one of perhaps infinitely many universes in an inconceivably vast multiverse. Most of those universes are barren, but some, like ours, have conditions suitable for life...The idea is controversial. Critics say it doesn't even qualify as a scientific theory because the existence of other universes cannot be proved or disproved. Advocates argue that, like it or not, the multiverse may well be the only viable non-religious explanation for what is often called the "fine-tuning problem"—the baffling observation that the laws of the universe seem custom-tailored to favor the emergence of life.[9]

Back to Hawking, let's try giving him the benefit of the doubt. Let's just say that the multiverse is a real possibility. However, a theory is only as good as its ability to explain all the data within its domain. And in this case, the domain is vast—the origin of all things. Consequently, the Multiverse Theory should be able to explain the origins of the laws of science, life, the cell, DNA, consciousness, free will, objective morality, and many other phenomena. Sadly, the multiverse is silent on all of these issues. Those who commend the multiverse must come up with an assortment of purely naturalistic explanations for all of these perplexities. Their only retort is feeble at best: "Science might not have the answer today, but someday it will." Truly, this is an example of great faith.

INTELLIGENT DESIGN

A skeptic once challenged me to give him a definition of intelligent design. I did, but he remained unimpressed. Therefore, I asked him to give me a definition of non-design, along with an example. He offered the cosmos:

- "My example is the cosmos. I have no comparison set to call it 'designed.' It is, of course, a provisional position until such a set has been found. But to me, it seems the most intellectually honest position to hold. I don't want to assume that a supernatural explanation must be the answer."

There is nothing inherently dishonest about ascribing the cosmos to supernatural causation. Furthermore, there is no evidential reason to suppose that the cosmos is not designed. In fact, there are a number of considerations that point quite clearly to the idea of design. Here are just a few that I shared with my friend:

- THE FIRST LAW OF THERMODYNAMICS—This law of science declares that neither matter nor energy is either created or destroyed. The fact that matter and energy are interchangeable and indestructible is a formidable affirmation for intelligent design. Interestingly, the Bible claims that after God created, He rested from His creative work. Consequently, matter/energy is no longer being created—or even destroyed.

  However, this "First Law" disqualifies the implicit naturalistic assumption of gradual development. It is interesting to note that while the majority of scientists believe in Darwinian gradualism—the gradual creation of new genetic information by random mutation—they understandably reject the idea of a gradual development of matter from nothing. Instead, they believe that all matter arose from a tiny ball, which magically exploded into what has become our universe, with all of its elegance, continuity, changeless laws, and design. But Who designed the "ball"? Who guided how it "exploded" into the greatest of all marvels…life?

- THE SECOND LAW OF THERMODYNAMICS—According to this law, objects do not form and come together from a state of chaos to order, as naturalism would require. Instead, the "natural" tendency is always moving towards a state of dissipation, or entropy.

- THE FINE-TUNING OF THE COSMOS— Could the elegant engineering of the universe have come about by chance, counting on probabilities which defy all odds? The likelihood of such a thing occurring defies chance.

- THE NOTION THAT LIFE COMES FROM NON-LIFE—
This idea supposes that life, consciousness, and free will could emanate from non-life. This is another postulate that defies all odds.

- THE IDEA OF SOMETHING COMING FORTH FROM NOTHING—This is a flat-out denial of science. It just cannot logically be true. Therefore, some *thing* or some *One* must be eternal and uncaused. If this were not the case, then we would encounter the problem of infinite regress. In other words, how far back the "chain" of causation can we move? Since both science and logic have determined that the universe is not eternal, this leaves only the Creator to fill that void.

I pressed my friend to give me just one clear example of something that was not designed. I knew I was on safe ground. I was absolutely positive that he would not be able to offer up even one instance of non-design. For one thing, it is logically impossible to rule out design. Scientists have discovered discernible patterns even in "chaos." Some naturalists offer snowflakes and crystals as examples of non-design. However, these examples from nature are merely replicating the design that is already infused into their chemistry. Instead, everything gives evidence of design. Even the simplest atom is a miracle of God's workmanship. Certainly, the immutable and elegant causal laws of science point emphatically to their Maker.

There are thousands of versions of the "Argument from Design," or, the "Teleological Argument." In fact, these arguments can take as many forms as there are objects in the cosmos. Consequently, this is the most common argument, because we are surrounded by examples of design wherever we look. However, these tokens of design are often quickly dismissed from any discussion by invoking the "god of the gaps" argument, to which I have already alluded. Here is the way it is generally stated:

- "Since we scientists do not yet have a naturalistic, scientific explanation for the origins of the universe, it is not scientifically warranted to fill this gap in our present understanding with the idea that 'God did it.' Such a conclusion ignores the fact that science has been trying to fill the gaps in our knowledge for a long time and will continue to do so."

However, for many reasons, this is not a scientific conclusion. The next chapter will deal with this challenge.

THE "GOD OF THE GAPS" FALLACY: AN IN-DEPTH LOOK

CHAPTER SUMMARY

The atheist charges that God has been relegated by theists into the ever-decreasing and shrinking gaps which remain in scientific knowledge. However, this pitting of science against God is fallacious. Instead, ID—intelligent design—is totally compatible with science.

What is the "God of the Gaps" argument? Here is how *atheism.wiki.com* explains it:

- God of the Gaps is a concept that comes from the fact that God is being squeezed into an ever-smaller series of existential gaps...At one time, all the phenomena in the universe could be ascribed to God. The stars, the rain, the seasons etc. With time, and improved scientific explanations, the number of things for which "God did it" was a good explanation was reduced, and god was equally reduced to inhabiting ever smaller gaps in human knowledge...It should be remembered however, the fact that science has no present explanation in no way means that god (or Uranus, Zeus, Odin or any other god/goddess) exists or that the God/Gods of any other Mythology exist. Indeed, if we were never to answer these questions it still wouldn't mean that Allah created the Universe or that Thor causes it to thunder.

Atheism hopes to demonstrate that any possible argument in favor of God is being pushed into increasingly narrow gaps or margins. These gaps would be the areas where science has not yet been able to provide an explanation. Atheists are hoping that once these areas have all been scientifically explained, there will remain no further argument or gap where God would be the obvious explanation.

However, there is a hidden and fallacious assumption that has co-opted science in favor of atheistic naturalism. Many assume that scientific findings disqualify rather than validate the existence of God. But could it not be possible that, properly understood, the existence of God could actually be validated by science itself?

This unfounded assumption is derived from another related logical error; namely, that the explanation for any given phenomenon must be *either* scientific *or* divine...and never both. This erroneously places science in opposition to God and intelligent design (ID). If you were to ask me why I ordered a Big Mac, I could simply say that I was hungry. But what if you responded: "No, it was because of your biological machinery..."? Then, my answer to you would be: "Why can't it be both?"

Science, as well as eating a Big Mac, rests on a multi-layered foundation. The real question or controversy we are dealing with is this: "Do natural, undesigned laws account for scientific knowledge? Or do designed, purposeful laws form the basis of what we know through science?" Instead of a conflict between God and science, the controversy is more a matter of causation. Is the ultimate cause naturalism or supernaturalism? Blind chance or intelligent design?

Of course, we cannot put God or intelligent design in a test tube. We are equally unable to put the concept of natural causation into a test tube. Both are *beyond direct experimentation and replication*. Instead, we must examine them from a higher, more philosophical perspective. We need to ask ourselves which theory best accounts for the findings. Is the answer to be found in naturalism or supernaturalism, a.k.a. intelligent design? Here are some considerations in favor of ID:

1. Although we all agree that objects are subject to laws and respond in formulaic and predictable ways, there is no evidence whatsoever that these laws are natural and unintelligent in origin or operation. Natural causation cannot be invoked to explain them; there was no unconscious, inanimate but eternally pre-existent

"natural" entity that caused the various "natural" laws. It is more likely that they find their origin and unity in the single, transcendent and eternal Mind of God.

2. Reason, logic, and the laws that govern this universe are unchanging. In an ever-expanding universe of molecules-in-motion, naturalism cannot account for them; that is, for their stability and permanence. Only an omnipotent, immutable God can. Only a transcendent, outside-of-this-universe God is impervious to change. Only an omnipotent and changeless God can account for the changeless laws of science.

3. Reason, logic, and the laws of science are uniform, wherever we look and in whatever historical period. Their influences are therefore predictable, whether we take measurements on Mercury or on the moon or on the earth. This suggests that these laws are transcendent. How so? Forces that we create are localized. Therefore, we find that their influence diminishes as the distance between objects increases. I can't pick up New York City's WQXR radio signal when I am in Pennsylvania. However, the laws of science operate uniformly, predictably, and universally...transcending the material constraints placed upon them by their location in the universe. Naturalism cannot account for this transcendence; supernaturalism affirms it.

4. The laws of science require an adequate cause, but naturalism is unable and unwilling to provide one. In fact, there are many things that naturalism cannot adequately explain: life, DNA, the fine-tuning of the universe, free will, consciousness, moral absolutes, and the unchanging physical laws, to name just a few. In order to theorize about the origins of these things, naturalism is compelled to take numerous wild, theoretical leaps, like those involved with the theory of the multiverse. However, these leaps are not evidentially-supported and violate the principle of simplicity—that the simplest

explanation is likely to be the best one. In contrast, intelligent design requires just one leap to an omnipotent Creator to explain all. He alone is marvelously sufficient in all things.

5. Our experience with causal agents informs us that the cause is always greater than the effect. If the effect were greater than the cause, it would suggest that some aspect of the effect had been uncaused, a scientific impossibility.

6. Naturalism cannot account for the elegance of the laws of science. Nor can it explain how those laws work in complete harmony, and without undermining one another. However, intelligent design can!

In the next few paragraphs, we will examine yet another shortcoming of naturalism—the fact that naturalism cannot explain how Darwinian gradualism can account for the irreducibly complex components of organisms.

GRADUALISM

Darwin offered "gradualism" as a way to explain the development of beneficial structures or components which improve a creature's ability to survive and reproduce. He theorized that each successive change had to confer a survival advantage in order for it to be "selected" and thus passed on by evolution. But there is a problem with this view. A new and adaptive structure, like sonar in dolphins, requires *numerous simultaneous changes* before it can confer any survival advantage. No evidence has ever been found to provide any clear proof of this occurring.

To enhance our understanding of this concept, let us consider an example from the world of insects. For a caterpillar to become a butterfly, it builds a cocoon around itself, totally deconstructs, and then it is transformed into an entirely different creature. For this to happen, thousands of pieces of genetic information must *simultaneously* exist beforehand. Without all of this information already in place, the caterpillar would die in its cocoon.

This brings us directly to the concept of "irreducible complexity," or, IC. According to the tenets of IC, unless all of the essential materials and information are simultaneously present in an organism, no new functioning structure can naturalistically arise.

The mouse trap is often used as an illustration. For a mousetrap to work, it cannot evolve gradually. All of the five parts must first be present and properly constructed for the trap to succeed at catching a mouse. If any one of those parts is missing, the trap will not work.

It has been said that every organ, structure, or component part of an organism is "irreducibly complex" and therefore defies evolutionary explanations. For example, our blood must be able to clot, or any cut can cause us to bleed to death. However, in order for this clotting to take place, there must be 12 specific individual chemicals reacting in a domino effect to form a clot.

Furthermore, these chemicals must be present in exactly the correct amounts if clotting is to occur. No animal could survive unless each and every required component was present from the start. This life-or-death reality defies any gradualistic Darwinian explanation.

Another example of irreducible complexity from the world of insects was offered up by Bruce Malone and Julie Von Vett. The carnivorous Venus flytrap provides an interesting case study. In order for "Venus" to survive on its exclusively insect diet, five complex systems must simultaneously be in place:

1. An insect—the potential meal—must be lured to Venus by a sweet-smelling aroma.
2. Venus must sense that the insect is there.
3. Venus must trap the insect.
4. Venus must have the digestive apparatus to digest the insect.

    5. Finally, Venus must be able to eliminate the remains.[1]

Each of these systems needs to be present simultaneously. Lacking any one of these IC processes would mean starvation, death and extinction for the Venus flytrap.

We encounter these same challenges to the viability of naturalism within each species. For yet another example, Malone and Von Vett cite the sea cucumber. It is able to survive its would-be predators by presenting and thus offering up its "sticky" organs, which are then able to effectively seal a predator's throat. The authors ask, rhetorically:

- How did the first sea cucumber survive the first time he spilled his guts? From the very beginning, he had to have the ability to vomit out his sticky organs and then have the ability to regrow them.[2]

Without all of these complex capabilities functioning simultaneously, the sea cucumber could not have survived.

Finally, Malone and Von Vett offer the example of the poisonous snake. In order for the snake's "weapon" to be functional, many systems have to be in place, all at the same time:

1. Venom
2. A gland for the storing of the venom
3. A canal to transfer the venom to the fangs
4. Hollow fangs…to inject the poison
5. Muscles to contract the venom reservoir
6. A nervous system to signal the muscles to contract
7. Spring-loaded fangs
8. Instincts to know when and how to use all these systems[3]

All of these processes must be present at the same time for the snake to deliver its lethal blow. If just one of them is lacking, the snake will not survive. Only the Design Hypothesis is capable of accounting for the simultaneous appearance and operation of all of the necessary systems.

❖ ❖ ❖

Is there a trace of any gradual change or adaptation in the fossil record? No. Yet evolutionists actually believe that mammals evolved from amphibians. The fossil record is deafeningly silent about any such transition.

Despite these findings, naturalists wrongly insist that ID rests on the faulty logic that its proponents are invoking God to mask their ignorance: "Since we don't understand it, God must have done it." This is a gross misrepresentation of the intelligent design hypothesis, which relies on facts and the common-sense notion that if something appears to be designed, *then it most likely is designed*. This stance becomes even more defensible when we find that the probability that random genetic mutations and natural selection can account for any organ of any creature is off-the-charts.

Most of us have very little difficulty detecting design. When we determine that a book, a Boeing 747, a watch, or a computer program is designed, we are standing on solid ground. We draw this conclusion based on the appearance of the detailed and functional design we see in each item. Therefore, when we consider a human being, it defies reason to suppose that our more than three billion bits of coordinated DNA—the language of life—just...happened.

This should be obvious, especially in light of the fact that evolution cannot even begin to explain DNA. Why not? DNA must *pre-exist life* before evolution can act upon it, let alone begin to explain its existence. Even the simplest life-forms require at least 500 different genes before they can exist and function properly. Evolution is incapable of influencing this code until the organism exists and can evolve through natural selection.

Moreover, there is no evidence that any biological life has ever existed without DNA. Nor is there any other code detailed enough to direct the construction of the simplest life-forms. Therefore, evolution cannot even begin to explain life, or DNA.

Chapter 9

Ironically, the naturalistic hypothesis concerning the origins of DNA, or of anything else, is vulnerable to the very same accusation it brings against ID: "Since we don't understand it, natural forces must have done it." This is a veritable "naturalism of the gaps," a farce doubly compounded by the fact that there is absolutely no evidence that anything has ever been caused naturally, without intelligent design.

ANOTHER FATAL FLAW
OF NATURALISM AND EVOLUTION

CHAPTER SUMMARY

Belief in God provides a survival advantage. From an evolutionary point of view, "erroneous" beliefs like this should prove disadvantageous.

Both naturalism and the theory of evolution maintain that, through natural selection, the human brain has evolved to a point where we have been given a number of survival advantages. We have been enabled to derive accurate data with our senses and apply adaptive thinking to what we observe in the world.

However, according to the naturalist, there are other aspects of our neurological wiring which produce irrational thinking. Belief in God is considered a primary example. Theologian and pastor, Timothy Keller, has written about the deficiency of such a view:

- Evolutionists say that if God makes sense to us, it is not because he is really there, it's only because that [irrational] belief helped us survive and so we are hard wired for it. However, if we can't trust our belief-forming faculties to tell us the truth about God, why should we trust them to tell us the truth about anything, including evolutionary science? If our cognitive faculties only tell us what we need to survive, not what is true, why trust them about anything at all?

- What is not fair is to do what so many evolutionary scientists are doing now. They are applying the scalpel of their skepticism to what our minds tell us about God but not to what our minds are telling us about evolutionary science itself.[1]

Keller is pointing out the inconsistency of evolutionary thinking, including one of its principal tenets, natural selection. Evolutionists assume that, through natural selection, all the adaptations we have made thus far have given us a survival edge...*except for our belief in God*. Naturalists regard belief as both irrational and outmoded for the enhancing of our ability to survive.

However, our beliefs and intuitions provide us with essential feedback. If we cannot trust our thoughts or intuitions about God, then how can we trust them about anything else? C.S. Lewis makes this point as he considers love and the enjoyment of music:

- You can't, except in the lowest animal sense, be in love with a girl if you know (and keep on remembering) that all the beauties both of her person and of her character are a momentary and accidental pattern produced by the collision of atoms, and that your own response to them is only a sort of psychic phosphorescence arising from the behavior of your genes. You can't go on getting very serious pleasure from music if you know and remember that its air of significance is a pure illusion, that you like it only because your nervous system is irrationally conditioned to like it.[2]

We instinctively know that our experiences with love and music are more than just a collection of meaningless biochemical reactions. According to Lewis, a naturalistic, meaningless universe does not accord with our intuitions and beliefs about it. As a result, we cannot live in any sort of harmony with a worldview like this. To do so, we would be compelled to either modify our worldview or dismiss our most basic intuitions.

Are we ready to dismiss these intuitions? They infuse our lives with meaning and fullness. Are we now to understand that they are feeding us a distorted, self-deluding message? Returning to Keller's point, if our brains are deluding us in certain areas, how can we trust that they are not deluding us in other areas—areas where our lives are enriched? Are we ready to regard our love for our wives, or our appreciation for certain pieces of music or art that moves us...as merely a set of biochemical reactions?

Naturalistic evolutionists also claim that our biochemically-determined perceptions and intuitions delude us in other ways. Our intuition that we are able to freely make choices is another supposedly irrational belief. Although we sense that we are making our own decisions, according to the naturalists, this is not the case. We might think that we are freely choosing a cheeseburger and fries at a restaurant, but instead what is actually happening is that our genes and our biochemistry are once again deluding us.

Are we mistaken? Have our genes deceived us? Are they using us as vessels through which they can enjoy a temporary survival advantage? If this is so, and if we should be in doubt about our free will, then of what else should we be in doubt? Maybe each one of us is not an individual at all but rather a part of some mass consciousness. Maybe we should doubt that the physical world actually exists. Perhaps our thoughts and perceptions are all imaginary, a mere dream. Such doubts would undermine our ability to get out of bed in the morning. And how could we hope to contribute anything of worth to the world with such a perspective? Yet this is the sort of dystopia where naturalistic skepticism would lead us.

❖ ❖ ❖

This same problem exists in the area of morality. Naturalism denies the existence of objective and absolute moral laws. According to naturalists, any sort of moral code is nothing more than another baseless but "adaptive" belief that our genes have imposed upon us. These skeptics claim that they don't need God to be good. At the same time, they reject that there is any objective basis or law for what is good or bad, just or unjust. Nevertheless, they still rely on the "common law" written by God upon the conscience of each of us. From their point of view, the conscience is merely a biochemical set of reactions, having nothing to do with any objective set of moral laws, let alone God.

Yet, based upon these moral "intuitions," naturalists correctly intuit, or feel, that when they violate their conscience, *they are violating absolute moral laws* and deserve punishment, just as Romans 1:32 declares. Likewise, we Christians know that there are times when we sense that Someone greater than we are is condemning us.

More to the point, naturalists are willing to trust in their moral intuitions or conscience, while they distrust their intuition that God exists.

Interestingly, naturalistic evolutionists believe that our intuition of the existence of God had, at one time, conferred on us a survival advantage. However, they are now convinced that the human race has transcended its need for this belief. Furthermore, these proponents of naturalism and evolution feel as if they are bestowing yet another survival advantage on the human race. How? By persuading others to also discard their outmoded beliefs, including any belief in God.

Because of the supposed strides in human evolutionary development, skeptics are unwilling to consider how our intuitions or beliefs could now give us any survival advantage. According to this line of thinking, our "deluded" human intuitions severely interfere with our ability to understand and make positive adjustments to our environment. But if we are as deluded as the naturalists suggest, how can we then trust anything regarding our thinking? How can we trust our instincts about human rights, justice, love, or compassion?

Besides, isn't it true that building costly temples to God, composing music, or even serving the poor might distract us from our "ultimate" goal of survival? If that is so, then should all such pursuits be abandoned? Furthermore, should such altruistic and other-directed efforts be discouraged because the sacrifices involved might lead to premature death? How could anyone be so foolish as to believe that there is actually something greater than one's own immediate welfare?

❖ ❖ ❖

In contrast to naturalism and other follies, the Christian worldview regards our intuitions as necessary guides and, consequently, beneficial for our ultimate well-being. These beliefs do not delude us any more than our ears or eyes delude us. Instead, they have the potential to enrich our lives immensely, far beyond mere survival. They allow us to experience depth, awe, the wonder of sunsets, the changing seasons, the enjoyment of food and music and friendship.

In fact, many studies suggest that Christians experience improved physical and mental health, improved family relationships, and even an enhanced enjoyment of sex. If Christian beliefs are out-of-step with reality, how can we explain such documented benefits? In the short run, rose-colored glasses might temporarily smooth over life's rough places. But in the marathon of life, such blinders will present us with a high price tag. There are consequences for baseless denials of truth, and likewise for beliefs which do not correspond to reality.

Where did these intuitions come from? Not from any blind, naturalistic process that cares nothing about us. Instead, they come from a God who does care! They enrich us with a sense of purpose and meaning. They even afflict us with guilt and shame when we violate His moral law, which is universally imprinted on our conscience. Furthermore, it is these same intuitions that provoke us to look beyond our immediate pleasures and pains.

In conclusion, what the naturalist regards as irrational and no longer necessary, we understand as part of a grand design. This grand design was written on our hearts by One who truly loves us and is intensely concerned about our welfare.

THE COSMOLOGICAL ARGUMENT FOR THE EXISTENCE OF GOD

CHAPTER SUMMARY

All things that have come into existence are caused to exist by other things. If there is no eternal, uncaused Causer, then nothing can exist. Conclusion: Therefore, there must be an eternal, uncaused Causer—God.

I think that formal logical presentations of an argument offer clarity and appeal. The next chapters are presented in the form of a syllogism—two premises and a conclusion. If the two premises are shown to be likely, then the conclusion is logically unavoidable.

For a common example of a syllogism:

> PREMISE #1: All bachelors are unmarried.

> PREMISE #2: John is unmarried.

> CONCLUSION: John is a bachelor.

It is easy to see that if we prove that John is unmarried, it automatically means that he is a bachelor.

Similarly, the Cosmological proof argues that any first Cause must have always existed or it too would have required a cause. Only God can fulfill this essential requirement. Here is what the syllogism looks like:

> PREMISE #1: All things that have come into existence have been caused to exist.

> PREMISE #2: If there is no eternal, uncaused Causer, then nothing could exist.

CONCLUSION: Therefore, there must be an eternal, uncaused Causer—God.

PREMISE #1:
All things that have come into existence have been caused to exist.

To deny this is absurd. To illustrate, if I tell you that my cup of coffee just appeared without any cause, you would think me crazy. This is because we never see any uncaused thing materialize out of nothing.

We reasonably assume that there are causes for any phenomenon. That is why we do science—to discover the relationship between what is caused and the agents that caused it. Therefore, to deny that phenomena require causes is to reject the basic assumption of science—that everything has a reason or a cause.

PREMISE #2:
If there is no eternal, uncaused Causer, then nothing could exist.

It follows that something or Someone must be uncaused—and therefore eternal—in order to explain the existence of everything else. Because this ultimate Causer is eternal, there is no need to explain its cause, because it always was.

We cannot conclude that the universe caused itself, because it would first need to have existed *before it could have caused anything else*. Nor can we conclude that there was an apparatus that caused the universe. Why not? Because, then we would have to ask, "What caused the apparatus?" If someone were to claim that there was a mechanism that caused the apparatus, then we would again have to ask, "What caused the mechanism?"

This is the problem of an "infinite regress" of causes or explanations. It means that, ultimately, there is no sufficient cause or explanation at the end of the line where the buck stops. The causal chain just keeps going back—infinitely—without any foundational, adequate, or original cause. Thus, no causal explanation of the universe could ever be adequate without an uncaused and eternal Causer.

The eternal cannot be a *something,* which means that the universe cannot be eternal. Matter and space cannot exist apart from time, and time could *not* have been eternal. Why not? The concept of eternity *requires an infinite number of years to have already passed* in order to ever arrive in the present—a logical impossibility. Why? Because only a finite number of years could possibly have passed to bring us into this moment! It is impossible for an infinite number of years to have already passed. Infinity knows no limits. If an infinite number of years had already passed, then that span of time would not have been infinite, but merely finite.

Therefore, the eternal Cause must be Transcendent. He must transcend time and space and exist apart from this time-bound universe. Once again, the eternal must be an eternal Some*one*, not at all any sort of some*thing*.

Big Bang cosmology also maintains that the universe—time, space, and matter—had a beginning in time. According to Stephen Hawking:

- Almost everyone now believes that the universe and time itself had a beginning in the Big Bang![1]

This has proven to be a bitter pill for most cosmologists. If the universe had a beginning, then, according to Hawking, that would open the door to a disturbing question: *"Who caused it?"* This is what Hawking had freely admitted about the now defunct steady-state theory of the universe—which posits that the universe has always existed:

- The motivation for believing in an eternal universe was the desire to avoid invoking divine intervention to create the universe and set it going.[2]

The law of entropy also argues against an eternal universe. By now, after a supposedly infinite amount of time has passed, everything in the universe should have fallen into a state of dissipation, or entropy. Another consideration: If the universe has been expanding infinitely, space and matter should also be infinite. However, modern science denies that any of these entities are infinite.

CONCLUSION:
Therefore, there must be an eternal, uncaused Causer—God.

This Causer must be an intelligent and eternal Being who transcends time, space, and materiality—a Being who has the causal power to produce everything else.

CHALLENGES

Many atheists, when confronted with these facts, hoist up the flag of agnosticism as a convenient way to dodge the truth. They argue that we know so little about cosmology that we should be careful and not embrace any conclusions.

While atheists and agnostics are correct about knowing so little, I think that the little that we do know points convincingly to God.

Other skeptics frequently bring up the God-of-the-Gaps argument: "When we don't really know the answers, you creationists always assume that God did it." This stance is a blatant misrepresentation of theistic proofs. Here's how:

1. We can just as easily charge the skeptic with Naturalism-of-the-Gaps: "Because we don't know...natural, unintelligent forces must have done it."

2. There does not exist one shred of evidence that causal agents operate naturally and without intelligence or purpose. Even the objects acted upon seem to be wonders of design, including the tiniest atom.

3. Theistic proofs do not conclude: "We don't know, so God must have done it." Instead, the proofs used by theists compare ID—intelligent design, or supernaturalism— with naturalism, and demonstrate that ID is the most reasonable conclusion.

Others charge that theistic proofs only make God seem probable and, therefore, should not serve as a basis for our faith and a relationship with God.

Actually, on this point, I agree. That is why I do not invoke theistic proofs as a basis for faith but for *the defense of faith*. These proofs are a potent means by which we may challenge the assaults of those who are skeptical of theism. Since I have a highly doubting disposition myself, I sometimes think through these proofs to silence my own doubts. This mental exercise helps me. I am reassured that I am following the path of truth.

BERTRAND RUSSELL
AND HIS REJECTION OF THE FIRST CAUSE
ARGUMENT FOR THE EXISTENCE OF GOD

Bertrand Russell, the author of *Why I Am Not a Christian*, was regarded as the most brilliant mathematician of his day. He wrote against the theistic proofs, including the "First Cause" argument for the existence of God. The First Cause is so closely related to the Cosmological Argument that I will be consolidating the two views as I deal with Russell's thinking on the subject. Here is the body of Russell's argumentation:

- [The First Cause argument for the existence of God] maintains that everything we see in this world has a cause, and as you go back in the chain of causes further and further you must come to a First Cause, and to that First Cause you give the name of God...If everything must have a cause, then God must have a cause. If there can be anything without a cause, it may just as well be the world as God, so that there cannot be any validity in that argument...There is no reason why the world could not have come into being without a cause; nor, on the other hand, is there any reason why it should not have always existed. There is no reason to suppose that the world had a beginning at all. The idea that things must have a beginning is really due to the poverty of our imagination. Therefore, perhaps, I need not waste any more time upon the argument about the First Cause.[3]

There are many problems with Russell's argument. He misconstrues the Cosmological Argument from the First Cause, writing in the previous paragraph: "If everything must have a cause, then God must have a cause." However, the major premise of the First Cause argument reads: "*Everything that begins to exist* must have a cause," leaving the eternal God out of the equation.

In fact, the argument from the First Cause posits that something or Someone must be eternal and uncaused. Without this uncaused first cause, there can never be a rational explanation for anything! Why not? Because cause "Z" requires a prior cause "Y," and "Y" requires an "X," and this would go on infinitely—a logical impossibility. Ultimately, what this means is that there is never a sufficient cause for anything.

Nevertheless, Russell did acknowledge that there is a need for something to be eternal and uncaused. But he suggested that the universe could be accepted as the uncaused cause with just as much validity as some might accept the idea of God. However, this suggestion violates both science and reason because science readily acknowledges that the time-space-matter universe did indeed have a beginning.

Robert Wilson and Arno Penzias, Nobel laureates in physics, initially believed in the "Steady State Theory," which maintains that the universe has always existed. If one begins with this premise, then the question, "Who created the universe?" becomes unnecessary. However, as the evidence began to accumulate against the "Steady State," Penzias admitted:

- The Steady State theory turned out to be so ugly that people dismissed it. The easiest way to fit the observations with the least number of parameters was one in which the universe was created out of nothing, in an instant, and continues to expand.[4]

Robert Jastrow was the founding director of NASA's Goddard Institute for Space Studies, a professor at Columbia University, and the director emeritus of the Mt. Wilson Observatory. Here is one of his observations:

- When a scientist writes about God, his colleagues assume he is either over the hill or going bonkers. In my case it should be understood from the start that I am an agnostic in religious matters. My views on this question are close to those of Darwin, who wrote, "My theology is a simple muddle. I cannot look at the Universe as the result of blind chance, yet I see no evidence of beneficent design in the details."[5]

It turns out that Jastrow does see scientific evidence for the existence of God. After strongly asserting his agnosticism, in one interview, he admitted…

- …that scientific evidence (including Hubble's discoveries) pointed quite clearly to the existence of a supernatural Creator. Yet, the materialistic philosophy he had long embraced rebelled at such a conclusion. He ended with an admission…: "I'm in a completely hopeless bind."[6]

Why the bind? Simply this: Jastrow remains committed to a naturalistic world view but sees the evidence pointing to ID. In *God and the Astronomers*, Jastrow also acknowledged that naturalism had failed to account for the evidence:

- At this moment it seems as though science will never be able to raise the curtain on the mystery of creation. For the scientist who has lived by his faith in the power of reason, the story ends like a bad dream. He has scaled the mountains of ignorance; he is about to conquer the highest peak; as he pulls himself over the final rock, he is greeted by a band of theologians who have been sitting there for centuries.[7]

This seems to rule out the possibility that the universe or any part of it could serve as our first cause. However, I think that the logical evidence against an always-existing-universe is even more damning. If the universe is eternal, it means that an infinite number of years would have needed to pass to ever arrive in the now, the present. Once again, this passage of time is a logical impossibility. Therefore, whatever is eternal—the first cause—*must lie outside of the time-space-matter continuum*. The first cause must transcend time, and this is exactly the portrait that the Bible presents of the Creator God:

- For thus says the One who is high and lifted up, who inhabits eternity, whose name is Holy: "I dwell in the high and holy place, and also with him who is of a contrite and lowly spirit, to revive the spirit of the lowly, and to revive the heart of the contrite." (Isaiah 57:15, ESV)

As a last resort, Russell asserted, "The idea that things must have a beginning is really due to the poverty of our imagination." Critics might just as easily retort that the idea of a beginning is due not so much to a poverty of our imagination as it is to a multitude of observations. So, perhaps there is a reality beyond our feeble imagination and even our logic. We live, believe, and make our decisions based upon the very limited knowledge that we possess at any given moment. We have nothing else. But to be responsible with our limited knowledge, experience, and the findings of science, we are obliged to conclude that the phenomena of this world do have both a beginning and a cause.

THE MORAL ARGUMENT
FOR THE EXISTENCE OF GOD

CHAPTER SUMMARY

Without God, moral absolutes cannot exist. Moral absolutes do exist. Conclusion: Therefore, God exists!

The moral argument for the existence of God is one of the most useful proofs. In fact, it bears repeating:

PREMISE #1: Without God, moral absolutes cannot exist.

PREMISE #2: Moral absolutes do exist.

CONCLUSION: Therefore, God exists!

PREMISE #1: Without God,
moral absolutes cannot exist.

Does the rejection of God also entail the rejection of any possible basis for objective moral truth? Atheist and former president and CEO of the Center for Inquiry, Ronald A. Lindsay, in one of the major tenets of his book—*Everybody Is Wrong About God*—argues that we do not need God to be good. At the same time, he understands that it is almost impossible to talk about being good...unless there already exists an objective good. And if God is rejected, what could be the basis of that which is good?

Many atheists have tried to put forward an objective starting point upon which to base their system of ethics. They might say something like the following: "Can't the objective moral good be based upon certain facts like, 'Pain must be a bad thing because people avoid being in pain'? Or, to flip the coin, that 'well-being—health—is a good thing'?" While we might feel that these things are true, without God, our feelings are no more than biochemical responses. Why then should they require that we do anything about them? Why should our biochemistry be our authority? Besides that, wouldn't our biochemical responses also coerce us to seek revenge, or to do other things that we feel are immoral?

The problem here involves jumping from what *is* to what *ought to be*. These are two separate issues. While it is true that we don't want pain and that we will automatically try to remove ourselves from it, that doesn't mean that we should remove all pain. For example, seeing a butterfly struggling to escape from its cocoon, a concerned passer-by might help the butterfly to escape. However, the butterfly needs to endure this essential, natural process and would die as a result of any intervention.

This whole discussion raises several fundamental questions:

✓ What makes life good?

✓ Does this world even contain an objective "good"? If we just made up this concept, why should we allow ourselves to be enslaved to it?

✓ Like the butterfly, perhaps we need the pain of struggle. But why should we struggle if there is no "good"?

✓ Could it be that we are all required to privately endure our own "karma"?

Applying these questions closer to home, the mere fact that our neighbor is suffering does not require us to do anything about it. Especially if we cannot even answer the fundamental question: Is it good to live? It might be pleasurable, but do we have an objective moral obligation to seek for the pleasure of others? Once again, compassion might lead us to this conclusion. But if compassion is no more than a biochemical reaction, why should we regard it as more authoritative than any other biochemical reaction, like seeking revenge? Perhaps, instead, an objective ethical belief system requires a higher moral authority—God. Ronald A. Lindsay acknowledged this problem:

- The difficulty in deriving moral obligations directly from discrete facts about the world was famously noted by the eighteenth-century Scottish philosopher David Hume, who remarked that from a statement about how things are—an "is" statement—we cannot infer a moral norm about how things should be—an "ought" statement...An 'is' statement and an 'ought' statement are distinct classes of statements.[1]

Lindsay concludes that we cannot logically jump from a fact to a moral obligation. In the same way as there is no moral connection between spilled milk and an obligation to clean it up, there is no moral connection between what "is" and what "ought to be." Something—an absolute moral directive—is clearly missing from this equation.

After surveying possible foundations for objective moral truth, Lindsay admits:

- So secular attempts to provide an objective foundation for morality have been... well, less than successful. Does this imply we are logically required to embrace nihilism [the belief that there is no objective moral truth, only our personal inclinations]?[2]

What, then, does Lindsay offer as an alternative to nihilism? First of all, it seems as if his understanding of morality is based on the day-to-day realities of our common human condition:

- We have vulnerabilities and needs similar to those of people who lived in ancient times and medieval times, and to those of people who live today in other parts of the world. The obligation to tell the truth will persist as long as humans need to rely on communications from each other. The obligation to assist those who are in need of food and water will persist as long as humans need hydration and nutrition to sustain themselves. The obligation not to maim someone will persist as long as humans cannot spontaneously heal wounds and regrow body parts. The obligation not to kill someone will persist as long as we lack the power of reanimation. In its essentials, the human condition has not changed much, and it is the circumstances under which we live that influence the content of our norms, not divine commands. Morality is a human institution serving human needs, and the norms of the common morality will persist as long as there are humans around.[3]

Thus, we see that Lindsay wrongly *assumes* that there is a moral bridge between the facts of our human condition and an innate moral imperative compelling us to take action for the welfare of others.

Meanwhile, other atheists have utterly abandoned the attempt to provide an objective basis for morality. Paul Kurtz—atheist, humanist, and author of *Humanist Manifesto II*—affirms that pragmatism is the only possible justification for morality:

- How are these principles [of equality, freedom, etc.] to be justified? They are not derived from a divine or natural law nor do they have a special metaphysical [beyond the material world] status. They are rules offered to govern how we shall behave. They can be justified only by reference to their results.[4]

While pragmatic, cost/benefit thinking can serve as a justification for living morally, the same pragmatism can be used to justify evil. Serial killer Ted Bundy confessed to over 30 gruesome murders. He explained his rationale before his execution:

- Then I learned that all moral judgments are 'value judgments,' that all value judgments are subjective [it just depends on how you think about them], and that none can be proved to be either 'right' or 'wrong'…I discovered that to become truly free, truly unfettered, I had to become truly uninhibited. And I quickly discovered that the greatest obstacle to my freedom, the greatest block and limitation to it, consists in the insupportable value judgment that I was bound to respect the rights of others. I asked myself, who were these 'others?' Other human beings with human rights? Why is it more wrong to kill a human animal than any other animal, a pig or a sheep or a steer? Is your life more to you than a hog's life to a hog? Why should I be willing to sacrifice my pleasure more for the one than for the other? Surely, you would not, in this age of scientific enlightenment, declare that God or nature has marked some pleasures as 'moral' or 'good' and others as 'immoral' or 'bad'? In any case, let me assure you, my dear young lady, that there is absolutely no comparison between the pleasure I might take in eating ham and the pleasure I anticipate in raping and murdering you. That is the honest conclusion to which my education has led me—after the most conscientious examination of my spontaneous and uninhibited self.[5]

Bundy's life demonstrates that pragmatism means different things to different people.

It can be argued that pragmatism's cost/benefit analysis is the lens through which we can best understand human history—not only its high points but also its lows. Therefore, pragmatism cannot serve as a replacement for objective moral truths.

The humanist Max Hocutt aptly observed that pragmatism and its cost/benefit analysis cannot fill this vacuum:

- To me [the non-existence of God] means that there is no absolute morality, that moralities are sets of social conventions devised by humans to satisfy their needs...If there were a morality written up in the sky somewhere but no God to enforce it, I see no good reason why anyone should pay it any heed.[6]

If an atheist truly wants to live pragmatically, she should try living her life as a Christian. Even atheists admit that such a life offers many pragmatic benefits. Occasionally, they will even confess, "I wish that I could have your faith." And yet, they are also quick to claim that "the truth" has to take precedence over any benefits.

Chapter 12

Lindsay argues that, even if God does exist, he cannot rationally be the basis for objective moral truth:

- ...we cannot possibly rely on God to tell us what's morally right and wrong. As Plato pointed out long ago in his dialogue Euthyphro, divine commands cannot provide a foundation for morality...Rules of conduct based on the arbitrary fiats of someone more powerful than us are not equivalent to moral norms. Moreover, it is no solution to say that God commands only what is good. This response presupposes that we can tell good from bad, right from wrong, or, in other words, that we have our own independent standards for moral goodness. But if we have such independent standards, then we don't need God to tell us what to do. We can determine what is morally right or wrong on our own.[7]

If we examine Plato's dialogue *Euthyphro*, we find Socrates asking Euthyphro, "Is the good loved by the gods because it is good, or is it good because it is loved by the gods?" In the first instance, God becomes irrelevant because the good exists apart from God. In the second instance, God's love for the good is arbitrary, and therefore not worthy of our moral consideration.

Let me try to restate this: If God DISCOVERS morality, then God is less than the morality He discovers. Thus, God is rendered unnecessary. If God CREATES morality and then imposes it upon us, He is an arbitrary despot.

What then is the solution? A third option: Morality is not arbitrary or independent of God, because it finds its origin within the Being of God. Besides, it is difficult to argue against God as the Source of objective moral law in favor of our own moral conscience or reason. After all, He has wired us with His own moral truths. Therefore, our conscience and reason is a replica of His. As a consequence, when we deny God, we also deny our own nature, our conscience and our reason, which were created in His likeness. Therefore, when we follow our God-given moral impulses, we are living in harmony and peace with these implanted truths. Furthermore, when we live this way, Christianity's pragmatic, well-documented benefits serve as circumstantial evidence.

While many concede that objective moral absolutes cannot exist without God, many will also deny that moral absolutes, like principles of justice, even exist. This brings us back into the clutches of nihilism. But as we will see in the next premise, moral absolutes do exist.

PREMISE #2: Moral absolutes do exist.

This premise is the battleground. How can we know that moral absolutes—moral laws—exist? We know they exist the same way we know that other laws exist. We perceive them. However, we perceive moral laws internally, while we perceive the laws of science externally. This means that the effects of moral laws cannot be precisely measured and calculated in the same way as the effects of gravity, for instance. In order to prove the existence of moral absolutes, we must examine ourselves and human behavior.

C.S. Lewis famously reasoned that making objective moral judgments is unavoidable:

- Whenever you find a man who says he does not believe in a real Right and Wrong, you will find the same man going back on this a moment later. He may break his promises to you, but if you try breaking one to him he will be complaining, "It's not fair."[8]

This same man might claim that it is just his DNA reacting. However, according to Lewis, his thinking and behavior betray something different:

- If we do not believe in decent behavior, why should we be so anxious to make excuses for not having behaved decently? The truth is we believe in decency so much—we feel the Rule of Law pressing on us so—that we cannot bear to face the fact that we are breaking it, and consequently we try to shift the responsibility.[9]

If the skeptic truly did not believe in objective moral truths—which he had violated—he would simply answer, "Well, those are *your* values, not mine. You have no right to impose them on me."

Upon closer examination, the skeptic's answer betrays the fact that even he believes in objective rights and wrongs. In what way? He shows no hesitation to accuse his accuser that he has "no right" to make his accusation.

At this point, the Darwinist might protest:

- I might react morally, but I *know* that this reaction is not a product of some higher truth hanging out there somewhere. This is merely the way that the forces of natural selection have biologically equipped our race. It's no more than an automatic, knee-jerk reaction. As a result, I don't see this as any proof for moral absolutes. Nor do I see this as proof that there is a God who is somehow setting the rules of the game. It's just a matter of our wiring!

On the contrary, it is far more than a mere knee-jerk reaction because of our "wiring."

Although the atheist claims that there is no absolute basis for judgment, he too judges as if he believes in absolute moral standards. Just watch the atheist for five minutes, and you will see that he agrees that his moral response is more than a knee-jerk reaction. How can I say this? The atheist passes judgments just as quickly as the theist. If someone were to push him, he would want an apology. He would *not* say this:

- Although I had this moral, automatic sort of response, I can't really hold you accountable for pushing me, since there are no absolute moral truths. Therefore, there are no objective rules of right and wrong which you have violated. So, I have no objective basis to judge your behavior. In fact, I am sorry. It was just my DNA acting up.

In the real world, the atheist would become indignant and would *remain* indignant long after his knee-jerk reaction had passed. This proves that he actually *endorses* the charge that he has been absolutely and objectively wronged. It is this endorsement, and not merely his unconscious response, that demonstrates that he too believes in an absolute moral law.

In fact, all of us believe in objective moral law. While we might deny it with our mouths, we affirm it with our behavior. What we do and the way we behave and react will always mock our assertion that "morality is just something we make up."

If we deny objective moral law, then we would be compelled to admit that rape, genocide, and torturing babies—although we might find these things distasteful—are not objectively wrong. In fact, with this mind-set, *nothing can be objectively wrong*. Furthermore, we would have to admit that good and bad, justice and injustice, exist only in our own minds.

However, if we were to adopt such a worldview, we would be condemning ourselves to a schizoid existence. While our heart tells us that torturing babies is absolutely wrong, our minds would try to convince us that such a belief is no more than a visceral reaction or a social construct that could be easily ignored.

With such a non-rational mindset, we would be saying "goodbye" to any hope for discovering meaning and purpose in life. In a world that is bereft of moral absolutes, there would be simply nothing meaningful for us to discover. In a mindless and meaningless universe, we would have to make up our meaning, our purpose, and our morality. We would have to play "make-believe," in opposition to what our heart—which knows otherwise—is whispering to us.

This was the subject of a secular discussion group I just attended. One atheist stated:

- I don't need a god to give me meaning. I *find* meaning when I see a mother with her baby and the love they share.

Perhaps he does "find meaning," but I also thought that there was something he was failing to recognize. Therefore, I responded:

- It seems to me that you too are acknowledging that life has a meaning *beyond what we create for ourselves*. You are not simply ascribing your compassion to meaningless, biochemical internal reactions. Instead, just as a Christian would, you are ascribing meaning to what your biochemically, materially-induced feelings are telling you. You see them pointing to something that transcends those reactions, which enlivens them with meaning.

Sadly, my atheist friend ignored the implications of my statement; he claimed that I didn't understand him.

His response is reflective of atheists in general. They are unable to live consistently with the materialistic implications of their beliefs— that nothing has any inherent meaning or objective moral significance. Furthermore, atheists are coerced to perceive meaning while denying its existence. They *know* that there are objective moral laws and a higher meaning that define us, even as they deny these truths.

Can blind, naturalistic processes account for the moral law imprinted upon our conscience? No. Can they account for the laws of science? Again, no. All laws, whether moral or scientific, demonstrate an elegance, a universality, and an immutability which point to a benign Designer.

❖ ❖ ❖

If we are honest with ourselves, we are able to see that an adherence to our internal moral "compass," or law, pays dividends. When we act in concert with its demands, we benefit and tend to feel at peace. For example, when we humble ourselves and apologize, we feel relief even if the other party refuses our apology.

Chapter 12

We might not believe that our moral struggles are anything other than an outdated biochemical reaction. But when we violate the moral law, we try to rationalize our bad behavior.

Meanwhile, self-help groups teach their members to be grateful—but to whom should they be grateful? "Well...just be grateful. Keep a journal and write down all the things you are grateful for." But why would people agree to such guidance? The answer is simple—they recognize the presence of an objective moral law.

People are also taught to forgive, but why? Because it pays psychological dividends. But is it right to forgive someone who has caused great harm? This question is not considered. Instead, in the world of "make-believe" values, we are told: "Just do it and stop asking questions about non-existent ultimate truth. It works, and that's enough. Just do it!" This is schizophrenic, a separation of mind from heart.

Mental health professionals recognize that living in accordance with our moral convictions is an important factor for mental health. Accordingly, Karen Wright wrote:

- Eudemonia refers to a state of well-being and full functioning that derives from a sense of living in accordance with one's deeply held values.[10]

This is obvious. Even skeptics perceive this and are intent upon living moral lives, even when they ascribe their moral programming to mindless evolution. However, they too know full well that they are playing "make-believe." They are intent on living virtuously but doubt the objective existence of virtue. So, how is it possible for virtuous living to be sustained among those who believe that virtue is only a construct of their own thinking?

Some, recognizing this problem, resort to the idea that we must live according to our nature. While there is some truth to this, our nature demands scrutiny. Should we be fearful of strangers, selfish, vengeful, unforgiving, or bitter merely because our nature has been "programmed" with these reactions? Of course not! Instead, we understand that our basic reactions have to be accepted or rejected based upon a higher criterion, our conscience.

Let me try to demonstrate this truth with another question: Why should we be altruistic? For the atheist, the only possible answer is pragmatic. Altruistic behavior works. It benefits, not only the recipient of such effort, but the one responsible for the work, as well. It all seems to be solely a matter of cost/benefit analysis. But is this actually the case? Altruism is not only a matter of positive outcomes. It is also about rock-solid convictions. Especially when it comes to our children, altruism often requires us to sacrifice for others, even to the point of the giving of our lives. Nothing pragmatic about that! Why then would we sacrifice ourselves? Because of the absolute moral truths we learn through our conscience, we know that there are some things that are more important than our own well-being.

Once again, even the skeptic will tell himself that he wants to live virtuously. However, to truly live this way requires him to relegate pragmatism to a lower priority, which he is willing to do. *He knows that it is right* to sacrifice even his life for the well-being of his family. At his core, he therefore knows that objective moral absolutes exist and that they trump pragmatic considerations. He knows that virtue exists, even as he verbally denies the existence of objective moral law.

Besides all this, moral absolutes also reflect a beautiful elegance of order and design in the same way that the law of gravity reflects elegance. When we wrong our wife, we feel guilty. When we apologize, we feel relieved, knowing that we have done the right thing. When she forgives us, we feel restored and encouraged, having learned an important lesson.

Even those who have committed horrendous deeds recognize this elegant design. Was Ted Bundy tormented by his deeds? Did he eventually repent of them? By his own admission, he did. Similarly, even our legal system has a demonstrated high regard for deathbed confessions. Why is this? Because our legal elites have noted a common pattern—that we are convinced of the truth of the moral law written on our conscience. In fact, we experience an overwhelming need to set the record straight as we face death. If we regarded these moral promptings as mere biochemical reactions, why would anyone even bother with them when facing a more overwhelming fate—death?

There is a common argument that people use to cast aspersions on the validity of objective moral truth. They bring up the idea that there is a diversity of moral expression when we compare one culture to another. However, I don't think that this objection argues against the existence of moral absolutes.

Let's take gravity as an example. We do not doubt that there is a very precise and elegant law of gravitation that allows us to predict how it will impact an object. However, there are many other factors that also impact how gravity affects a particular object—its mass, its shape, and the atmospheric conditions and location relative to other objects. For example, gravity makes certain objects rise—like a helium balloon. Gravity makes other objects fall, relative to their weight in comparison to the surrounding atmosphere—like a hammer. However, because of these variations in the ways that objects react, we do not dismiss the existence of the law of gravitation. We simply acknowledge that there are many other factors at play.

The same line of reasoning pertains to objective moral laws. Yes, culture and psychology also have an impact on the formation and expression of morality. But these relative factors do not argue persuasively against the existence of the moral absolutes.

CONCLUSION: Therefore, God exists!

We acknowledge an objective moral law in our heart and in our actions, even when we would rather not. Although harder to measure and predict, moral law is an inescapable reality, as real as gravity. While the skeptic's mouth might strenuously deny this reality, his heart disqualifies what his mouth is saying and will not allow him to believe otherwise.

Maybe there is a good reason to believe what life compels us to believe.

THE ARGUMENT FOR GOD FROM THE CONSCIENCE AND THE NEED TO BE TRUE TO OURSELVES

CHAPTER SUMMARY

While many regard their conscience as inviolable, they fail to see that they do so by assuming that the dictates of the conscience have a transcendent moral basis. This transcendent moral basis can only be justified if there is a God.

For many, the moral argument for the existence of God doesn't work. Such people simply deny the existence of objective moral laws and are willing to accept that there is nothing objectively wrong with rape, or even genocide. They are willing to live with the consequences of moral relativism. However, many of these same people will, nevertheless, claim that we must live according to the dictates of our conscience. This "Argument for God from the Conscience" might, therefore, speak to them.

In the *Handbook of Christian Apologetics*, Peter Kreeft and Ronald Tacelli—both of whom I will refer to as "K/T"—observe:

- Isn't it remarkable that no one, even the most consistent subjectivist, believes that it is ever good for anyone to deliberately and knowingly disobey his or her own conscience? Even if different people's consciences tell them to do or avoid totally different things, there remains one moral absolute for everyone: never disobey your own conscience.[1]

Remarkably, subjectivists and those of like mind regard their conscience as an absolute authority. But what is it about our conscience that gives it such authority that we would obey it? K/T list four possible sources for the authority of conscience:

1. The authority of the conscience from something less than me—nature
2. The authority of the conscience from me—the individual
3. The authority of the conscience from others equal to me—society
4. The authority of the conscience from something above me—God

Kreeft and Tacelli show that the first three possible sources fail to provide a basis for the absolute authority of our conscience.

1. The authority of the conscience from something less than me—nature...

K/T's comment:

- How can I be absolutely obligated by something less than me...?[2]

Certainly, a TV show or the song that my neighbor is singing cannot obligate me to do anything. Even less, I am not obligated by a message that flashes across my computer screen. How then could it be possible that such an impersonal and accidental thing as nature might have authority over me? The rain, the wind, the cows grazing in a field—nothing in the realm of nature should be able to run my life. Instead, there must be a greater authority.

2. The authority of the conscience from me—the individual...

K/T's comment:

- How can I obligate myself absolutely? Am I absolute? Do I have the right to demand absolute obedience from anyone, even myself? And if I am the one who locked myself in this prison of obligation, I can also let myself out.[3]

Clearly, there is no reason why my conscience, words, or decisions should be honored as the absolute authority of my life. If I make decisions, I can change my mind. I can break my promises. What binds me to my own words? Nothing! Besides all this common-sense reasoning, we must also admit that the decisions we have made have often been wrong.

If our conscience is merely a mindless set of biochemical reactions, it cannot serve as our absolute authority. Instead, any authority that our conscience has must come from a greater Source, just as a TV brings us messages that originate from beyond itself.

3. The authority of the conscience from others equal to me—society...

K/T's comment:

- How can society obligate me? What right do my equals have to impose their values on me? Does quantity [the majority] make quality?[4]

We might decide to follow a given law, but not because it possesses absolute authority. Instead, we recognize that our laws are evolving and can be challenged. If they were absolute, they would not be able to be contested, or amended. The fact that we can challenge them suggests also that we have authority over and are superior to them.

❖ ❖ ❖

Thus, we can see that the first three arguments that contend that our conscience is absolute and should never be violated have failed. There remains only one other option—that our immutable and all-wise God provides that foundation. Only He can provide the rationale whereby we can regard our conscience as absolute and inviolable.

It is ironic that the very Being we seek to avoid pops up despite all of our efforts to hide from Him, even as we exalt our conscience. Of course, when we realize, once again, that we are looking into the face of God by exalting our conscience, we might attempt to diminish its standing in order to escape from Him. However, this is His world and there is nowhere to run. Besides, we are created in His likeness (Ephesians 4:23-24). Therefore, to escape Him is to reject our very personhood.

When we reject His fatherhood and authority, we are also rejecting the authority of our conscience, which was given to us by God. In this way, we reduce ourselves to mere sophisticated machines, lacking any enduring value apart from our performance.

As if this degradation of our humanity were not enough, to reject God is also to reject free will and objective morality. Without an objective and authoritative law-Giver, there is no rational basis for objective morality or for any objective meaning or purpose for our lives. Instead, we are reduced to animalistic instincts and the pursuit of mindless pleasures. As a result, we often hear the misguided advice, "You have to find what feels right for you." This is no less than a denial of any higher and guiding truths.

The negative repercussions are numerous. Psychologist James Hillman made this poignant observation:

- We dull our lives by the way we conceive them...By accepting the idea that I am the effect of...hereditary and social forces, I reduce myself to a result. The more my life is accounted for by what already occurred in my chromosomes, by what my parents did or didn't do, and by my early years now long past, the more my biography is the story of a victim. I am living a plot written by my genetic code, ancestral heredity, traumatic occasions, parental unconsciousness, societal accidents.[5]

When we fail to embrace God, the One who has given us food, drink, family, identity, and life, we fail to embrace ourselves and our inherent dignity. What we had once regarded as inviolable—our

116

conscience—we are compelled to degrade to the status of a loud and troubling vestigial organ. Thus, we have doomed ourselves to a life of endless wandering, looking for our place...which we have already rejected.

Chapter 14

A PROOF OF GOD FROM THE LAWS OF PHYSICS

CHAPTER SUMMARY

The laws of physics are immutable, universal, and elegant. ID, or supernaturalism, is a better explanation for these observations than naturalism. Conclusion: An intelligent Designer must exist.

There are many weighty proofs for the existence and character of God. This is just one more of the many. Here it is presented in our familiar format:

PREMISE #1: The laws of physics are immutable, universal, and elegant.

PREMISE #2: ID—intelligent design, or supernaturalism—is a better explanation for observations from the laws of physics than naturalism.

CONCLUSION: An intelligent Designer—ID—most likely exists.

PREMISE #1: The laws of physics are immutable, universal, and elegant.

THE LAWS OF PHYSICS ARE IMMUTABLE: This should be obvious. If they were in flux, any scientific conclusion or description would be impossible, along with any replication of findings. Textbooks would have to be continuously changed and then discarded. Predictions could not be made. Any form of science would be impossible. Furthermore, there is no way to account for the immutability of the laws of physics, especially when we are dealing with a universe that is always expanding and changing. Therefore, these laws must be transcendently based, requiring a maintaining force outside of the universe.

118

THE LAWS OF PHYSICS ARE UNIVERSAL: This too should be obvious. It is only because these laws are universal that we are able to say anything about other galaxies, planets, stars, light, or anything else within the domain of science. The universality of these laws ensures us that the findings of scientists in China should match those of researchers in California.

THE LAWS OF PHYSICS ARE ELEGANT: This is equally obvious when we observe the elegance and simplicity found in the equations and formulas of physics:

- **G** = 8 *pi* **T**

This is Einstein's field equation. It is the cornerstone of his general theory of relativity, relating the gravitational tensor **G** to the stress-energy tensor **T** in a deceptively simple equation.

Many such elegant and precise formulas exist. The following is the formula for the gravitational attraction between two bodies:

- Gravitational Attraction = 1/ (distance between two bodies)^2

Here's how it works. Let's say that someone weighs 100 pounds on the surface of the earth, which is 4,000 miles from the center of the earth. If that same person were twice as far from the center $(2x^2)$, he or she would weigh 25 pounds! About this apparent elegance, Donald DeYoung wrote:

- Scientists have long wondered about the factor of [superscript] **2** in this expression. It simply looks "too neat." In an evolved universe, one would not expect such a simple relationship. For example, why isn't the distance factor 1.99 or 2.001? The gravity force has been repeatedly tested with sensitive torsion balances, showing that the factor is indeed precisely **2**...Any value other than **2** would lead to an eventual catastrophic decay of orbits and of the entire universe.[1]

Such precision cannot be the product of chance or of any effect due to an explosion we call the "Big Bang." Nor is this formula unusual in its beauty and elegance. The whole world of physics speaks of a *Design* and therefore, a *Designer*.

Take, for example, the world's most well-known formula:

- $E = MC^2$ (Energy = Mass x Speed of Light Squared)

Once again we find the same elegance and precision. The speed of light must be precisely squared. This formula demonstrates the harmonious interconnectedness of various physical elements—energy, mass and the speed of light. Such harmony defies the idea of a random creation set in motion by an explosion.

Here is what astronomer Fred Hoyle had to say about this and other random processes, including evolution:

- The chance that higher life forms arose by evolutionary processes is comparable with the chance that a tornado sweeping through a junkyard might assemble a Boeing 747 from the material therein.[2]

Nevertheless, intelligent people continue to believe in the "junkyard to Boeing" theory.

Without such elegance and simplicity, all the scientific laws that we know would have been undiscoverable and incomprehensible.

PREMISE #2:
ID—intelligent design, or supernaturalism—
is a better explanation for these observations
from the laws of physics than naturalism.

As he considered the origins of the universe and the laws of science, physicist Alexander Vilenkin believed that something was definitely "...in place beforehand—namely—the laws of physics." However, he admits:

- It's a great mystery as to where the laws of physics come from. We don't even know how to approach it.[3]

Perhaps Vilenkin doesn't know how to "approach it" because he is starting with the wrong paradigm. Certainly, from a naturalistic, atheistic perspective, this question is truly a "great mystery." However, this might be *more* than a mystery—it could be a veritable *impossibility* to find the answers to these big questions, on the basis of science alone:

1. The laws of physics are elegant, universal, and immutable. Only a cause of equal or greater magnitude could explain their existence and uniform functioning. This consideration alone should eliminate naturalism as a viable explanation.

2. A natural explanation for the origins of the universe is impossible because natural causation was not yet in existence at the beginning...to cause the "natural" laws. *Nothing* was as yet in existence in the universe!

3. Invoking any natural cause would also suffer from the problem of infinite regress: What causes the cause, and then, what causes the cause of the cause, *ad infinitum*? The only way to avoid this conundrum is to invoke the transcendent—an eternal Causer who doesn't require a cause.

4. It is also hard to understand how the unchanging laws of physics could arise from what is always changing. It is equally hard to envision how these laws could remain unchanged in our ever-expanding universe of molecules-in-motion.

5. There does not exist even a shred of evidence that anything has ever happened naturally; that is, without intelligence.

❖   ❖   ❖

IMMUTABILITY: Once again, in a universe of molecules-in-motion, it is hard or impossible to account for the unchanging-ness and origin of the laws of physics. Explosions—like the Big Bang, for instance—do not create laws, let alone immutability. It is therefore more likely that these laws have a Transcendent origin, arising in the Mind of God. This immutable Mind can account for immutable laws and their stability in the midst of change. They affect everything, but nothing affects them.

UNIVERSALITY: Causation within our universe is all localized. The further that we travel away from a radio station, the weaker the signal or reception. The further away from a bonfire, the less the warmth. However, the laws of physics operate uniformly and universally throughout the universe. These laws work the same in the Milky Way as they do in another galaxy. It is easier to account for this as a supernatural phenomenon rather than as a natural one. In fact, it seems that the laws of physics must have originated in a transcendent, rather than a physical, realm.

ELEGANCE: There is absolutely no natural mechanism that can account for the elegant and knowable design of the laws of physics. Explosions do not create immutable elegance.

Of course, it could be argued that at the present time, we are simply unaware of natural forces that might account for these laws. While this is true, such a proposal faces major obstacles:

1. There is absolutely no evidence that anything happens because of natural, un-designed laws.

2. Postulating such a collection of possible natural laws strains credulity and seems so much less likely than the postulation of a single Creator God.

3. The naturalistic explanation is no explanation at all. It is merely passing the buck to another set of natural laws which also require a causal explanation. Even if a natural mechanism could be identified that creates and maintains natural laws, it too would require its own

explanation. This leads to the formidable problem of an infinite regress.

4. Causes are always greater than their effects. If a cause is less than its effect, it means that some aspect of the effect is uncaused—a real conundrum for science.

5. Some argue that there might be a single, eternal and natural cause that causes all of the other laws of science. However, those who ascribe to this idea are merely replacing "God" with a natural creator having all the powers that God has—but without the ability to produce even one atom out of nothing.

Instead, an intelligent and eternal Designer/Creator is greater and has more explanatory power than any mindless cause. Therefore, ID can better account for phenomena like the laws of physics, the fine-tuning of the universe, life, intelligence, and consciousness...than what any unintelligent causation could provide—if indeed such a cause even exists.

CONCLUSION:
An intelligent Designer—ID—most likely exists.

A PROOF OF GOD FROM REASON

CHAPTER SUMMARY

Reason exists. Reason requires a transcendent Intelligence. Conclusion: A transcendent Intelligence must exist.

I enjoy taking snapshots of the glorious work of God. The one below is an example of reason/logic. All of these snapshots point back to the existence of the Creator. Once again, in the form of a syllogism, here's how:

PREMISE #1: Reason/Logic exists.

PREMISE #2: Reason/Logic requires a transcendent Intelligence.

CONCLUSION: A transcendent Intelligence must exist.

PREMISE #1: Reason/Logic exists.

This hardly requires any support. In fact, any argument against the existence of reason requires the use of reason, thereby contradicting itself. Therefore, nothing coherent can be uttered against the existence of reason or logic.

PREMISE #2: Reason/Logic requires a transcendent Intelligence.

There are several reasons for this. Reason is absolute, universal, and immutable. It *must* be immutable. If it isn't, it would be like trying to measure a room with maple syrup—a very unreliable, fluctuating measuring tool. Without the immutability and thus the stability of reason, there could be no truth, learning, or science.

Reason must also be universal or it would change from region to region. If reason were not universal, what would be reasonable in Alaska might not be reasonable in South Africa. It might mean that

Chapter 15

2 + 2 = 4 in Alaska but not in South Africa. The idea of what counts for reason could vary even from household to household. This would make learning and any form of acquiring knowledge impossible.

There seems to be a fortuitous fit between our reason and our world. The world is as amenable to reason as it is to mathematics.

But what would happen if reason worked according to different principles? If that were the case, would we be able to wrap our minds around the physical world in order to navigate it? Of course not!

These qualities cannot be accounted for by a universe of molecules-in-motion. They can only be accounted for by an immutable and universal Cause—something that transcends this universe and makes it amenable to an immutable and universal set of logical laws.

Reason is like the operating system—the software. The computer is what we refer to as the hardware. Both parts of the computer have to be intelligently created. If there is just one mistake in the software program, the facts and the data which have been entered cannot be properly tabulated and compared.

The software is comparable to our logic and reason. If they are not properly calibrated to the world of facts, we will not be able to comprehend what has been presented to us. Can logic and reason simply be constructed by our minds as we interact with the external world? This is unlikely. It is the software that organizes the data, not the data organizing the software. The "software" of our logic and reason must already be in place in order for us to learn, organize, and make use of the data that our sensory system feeds into us.

While it is true that humans created operating systems, humans could not have created reason. Reason predates humanity just as matter and energy predate humanity, since they are necessary for humanity's existence. Moreover, the operating system of a computer must be intelligently fine-tuned if it is to be functional. Amazingly, our capacities for reasoning seem to have also been intelligently fine-tuned to both our brains and the way the world works.

Besides, humanly-created systems are always being improved, whereas reason remains as is. Yet that same reason is adequate for all of our enterprises, no matter where we might choose to use it.

CONCLUSION:
A transcendent Intelligence must exist.

This same proof can be constructed for every law of science. *All of them* are elegant, immutable, and universal. *All of them* reflect a Supreme Intelligence. *All of them* defy any natural explanation of their origin or operation.

The Apostle Paul used this proof with the Athenian philosophers. He reasoned that the cause had to be greater than the effect. Therefore, we and our reason and logic could not have arisen from stone idols:

- "Being then God's offspring, we ought not to think that the divine being is like gold or silver or stone, an image formed by the art and imagination of man." (Acts 17:29)

Today, we have chosen for ourselves an idol even less substantial than those that are formed from gold or silver—a faith that this universe arose out of nothing, from previously non-existent natural causes, and incapable of creating even a single atom.

A TENTATIVE PROOF FOR GOD BASED UPON QUANTUM FINDINGS

CHAPTER SUMMARY

The universe is not material. It is mind-dependent, but the human mind cannot account for the universe. Conclusion: Therefore, there must be a greater mind—God!

I am not a scientist. I cannot personally vouch for the "findings" of science. Therefore, this proof is very tentative and based upon a *consensus* regarding the quantum world. The proof goes like this:

> PREMISE #1: The universe is not fundamentally material but mind-dependent.

> PREMISE #2: The human mind cannot account for the stability of the universe.

> CONCLUSION: Therefore, there must be a greater Mind—God!

PREMISE #1: The universe is not fundamentally material but mind-dependent.

Many now question whether the physical world is comprised of tiny particles, as was once widely believed. Arjun Walia, known for his work on the documentary, *The Collective Evolution III: The Shift*, observes:

- Quantum physicists discovered that physical atoms are made up of vortices of energy that are constantly spinning and vibrating, each one radiating its own unique energy signature…Again, what quantum mechanics reveals is that there is no true "physicality" in the universe, that atoms are made of focused vortices of energy-miniature tornadoes that are constantly popping into and out of existence. The revelation that the universe is not an assembly of physical parts, suggested by Newtonian physics, and instead comes from a holistic entanglement of immaterial energy waves stems from the work of Albert Einstein, Max Planck, and Werner Heisenberg, among others.[1]

Science is discovering that the "material" world is at least somewhat mind-dependent. I will share more of this startling idea in my comments on PREMISE #2.

PREMISE #2: The human mind cannot account for the stability of the universe.

Perhaps the basic building blocks of this physical world are thoughts. This idea, at least on the micro level, seems to be widely accepted among quantum physicists:

- A fundamental conclusion of the new physics also acknowledges that the observer creates the reality. As observers, we are personally involved with the creation of our own reality. Physicists are being forced to admit that the universe is a "mental" construction. Pioneering physicist Sir James Jeans wrote: "The stream of knowledge is heading toward a non-mechanical reality; the universe begins to look more like a great thought than like a great machine. Mind no longer appears to be an accidental intruder into the realm of matter; we ought rather hail it as the creator and governor of the realm of matter."[2]

In his own way, James M. Kushiner affirms what Sir James said in the previous citation:

- Every prediction quantum theory makes has been tested with consistent results... A photon, for example, may be either a wave or a particle state, but which it appears to be depends on a choice made by the observer...Some scientists like John Wheeler...have reached tentative conclusions:

"Useful as it is under everyday circumstances to say that the world exists 'out there' independent of us, that view cannot longer be upheld. There is a strange sense in which this is a 'participatory universe.'"[3]

Although we might be participants, there must also be a major figure acting as a Referee of some sort. If the human mind is able to impact external reality, there clearly seem to be severe limitations in place. For example, we do not seem to be able to impact gravity, the expansion of the universe, or the laws of physics. I can't even get my wife to think like me! Certain realities of this universe seem to be universal and immutable and impervious to our thinking. The seven billion inhabitants of the Earth tend to think about the universe in a multiplicity of very different ways. Yet the universe continues to move forward in a harmonious and predictable manner.

Any doubt about this should be dispelled when we consider the fact that the laws of physics pre-dated our own existence. Our thinking, therefore, cannot account for them.

Therefore, if the universe is mind-dependent, there must exist a greater Mind than ours—omnipotent and unchanging—which is singly responsible for the order and stability of the cosmos.

CONCLUSION:
Therefore, there must be a greater Mind—God!

If the universe is not fundamentally material but mind-dependent, then an all-determining Mind must be its Source and Sustenance.

What mind could possibly account for the laws of science, the fine-tuning of the universe, and the fortuitous conditions that are necessary for life and discovery? Only an all-intelligent and omnipotent One!

Even if we subsequently discover that this world is not mind-dependent, we still have to account for the myriad appearances of design, functionality, elegance, and fine-tuning we see all around us. And this brings us back to an omnipotent and omniscient Creator God, the very God described in the Bible.

Chapter 17

A FAILED PROOF AGAINST THE EXISTENCE OF GOD: THE PROBLEM OF HELL

CHAPTER SUMMARY

Eternal punishment is not just. The God of the Bible promises to punish with eternal torment. Conclusion: The God of the Bible cannot be just…or even exist.

The most serious philosophical charge brought against God is the charge that eternal punishment is unjust. It is part of an even broader challenge—the problem of evil and suffering. It goes like this:

- If the God of the Bible is just, loving, and omnipotent, He would not allow the death of babies, or suffering in general.

An answer to this challenge can be found in the words of Paul:

- I consider that our present sufferings are not worth comparing with the glory that will be revealed in us. (Romans 8:18)

If the tribulations and griefs of this life are no more than a moment compared to a blissful eternity, Paul's revelation offers a reasonable reprieve from the problem of evil and suffering. Furthermore, the Bible assures us that God has good reasons for allowing this evil for a limited time.

However, this does not answer the problem posed by the doctrine of "eternal punishment." For one thing, it doesn't seem right that God would *eternally* punish us for sins we committed within our fleeting, ephemeral lives. The famous atheist Robert Ingersoll (1833-1899) made this charge:

- Eternal punishment must be eternal cruelty and I do not see how any man, unless he has a brain of an idiot, or the heart of a wild beast, can believe in eternal punishment.[1]

Put less crudely, the atheistic argument goes like this:

> PREMISE #1: Eternal punishment is not just.
>
> PREMISE #2: The God of the Bible promises eternal punishment.
>
> CONCLUSION: The God of the Bible cannot be just…or even exist.

PREMISE #1: Eternal punishment is not just.

Admittedly, this challenge is difficult to address. Part of the difficulty lies in the challenge of nailing down the precise nature of eternal punishment. For one thing, there is the problem of figurative language. For example, skeptics charge that they will not believe in a God who is "stoking the eternal fires of hell." Even "Christian" evolutionists question the just nature of the God of the Bible. Karl Giberson, former co-head of *The Biologos Foundation,* which is devoted to selling evolution to the church, quoted and affirmed the words of the atheist Richard Dawkins:

- [The OT God is a] "tyrannical anthropomorphic deity… [who] commanded the Jews to go on genocidal rampages"…But who believes in this [OT] deity any more, besides those same fundamentalists who think the earth is 10,000 years old? Modern theology has moved past this view of God.[2]

Giberson did not mention his disdain for an eternal punishment. However, it seems likely that his understanding of and preference for "Modern theology" would also lead him and many supposedly Christian evolutionists to question the NT teachings on eternal punishment. The following are some questions about eternal punishment that I will try to answer…

Chapter 17

Does God proactively torment unbelievers with fire? I doubt it. It seems that much of the language of eternal fire is figurative rather than literal. In the same way, there are times when Jesus refers to hell as "outer darkness":

- "Then the king told the attendants, 'Tie him hand and foot, and throw him outside, into the darkness, where there will be weeping and gnashing of teeth.'" (Matthew 22:13; also, 8:12; 25:13. Verses including references to fire may be found in Matthew 13:42, 50)

Clearly, both the language of eternal fire and outer darkness cannot be taken literally—they are mutually exclusive. Besides, there are other verses describing what is associated with darkness or fire—"the weeping and gnashing of teeth"—as being associated with neither fire nor darkness, but of eternal regret:

- "*There will be weeping there, and gnashing of teeth*, when you see Abraham, Isaac and Jacob and all the prophets in the kingdom of God, but you yourselves thrown out." (Luke 13:28)

In this verse, "weeping...and gnashing" is not the product of darkness or fire but a reaction to the eternal loss of blessing. This would lead us to believe that eternal torment might not be the product of God proactively tormenting these unfortunate souls, but rather the angst-filled recognition of eternal loss.

Isn't it unjust of God to punish all of the lost souls with exactly the same punishment? On the contrary, it is apparent that there will be degrees of punishment:

- Then Jesus began to denounce the cities in which most of his miracles had been performed, because they did not repent. "Woe to you, Korazin! Woe to you, Bethsaida! If the miracles that were performed in you had been performed in Tyre and Sidon, they would have repented long ago in sackcloth and ashes. But I tell you, it will be more bearable

for Tyre and Sidon on the day of judgment than for you."
(Matthew 11:20-22)

Judgment will depend upon the amount of evidence for believing
that each of us receives from God (John 15:22, 24). Nevertheless,
according to the Apostle Paul, we all have some degree of
evidence, or light (Romans 1:18-20; 2:14-15). However, we reject
that light (John 3:19-21).

**What about the fate of babies or the aborted pre-born? What
evidence for believing could they possibly have been given?**
The Bible does not answer this question. However, it does teach
that the extent of punishment will be relative to the extent of our
guilt—what we knew and what we did:

- "That servant who knows his master's will and does not get
  ready or does not do what his master wants will be beaten
  with many blows. But the one who does not know and does
  things deserving punishment will be beaten with few blows.
  From everyone who has been given much, much will be
  demanded; and from the one who has been entrusted with
  much, much more will be asked." (Luke 12:47-48)

Although these verses do not explicitly lay out the punishment that
each one deserves, they do teach us that God will judge fairly,
taking into account individual situations.

Could it be that we choose our own eternal punishment? There
are also other considerations that make it difficult for us to
determine the exact nature of eternal punishment. In fact, it seems
Biblically possible that *hell and our condemnation might be self-
chosen:*

- "For God did not send his Son into the world to condemn the
  world, but to save the world through him. Whoever believes
  in him is not condemned, but whoever does not believe
  stands condemned already because he has not believed in
  the name of God's one and only Son. This is the verdict
  ["condemnation," KJV]: Light has come into the world, but

men loved darkness instead of light because their deeds were evil. Everyone who does evil hates the light, and will not come into the light for fear that his deeds will be exposed." (John 3:17-20)

Many verses inform us that Jesus did not come to judge (John 5:45; 8:15; 12:47-49; Matthew 7:2). How then is the unbeliever condemned? He is *self*-condemned! How can this be? Referring back to John 3: "...whoever does not believe stands condemned already because he has not [he has *refused* and has not] believed (John 3:18)." Once again, verse 19 reconfirms that judgment is a *self*-judgment. The unbeliever has the light, but he rejects the light in favor of the darkness. He hates the light and will flee from it.

Will this same condemnation accompany the unbeliever into the next life and before the great judgment? It seems so. Many verses assure us that those who reject the light will not be able to stand before it...or Him:

- Not so the wicked! They are like chaff that the wind blows away. Therefore the wicked will not stand in the judgment, nor sinners in the assembly of the righteous. (Psalm 1:4-5; also 15:1-2 and 24:3-4; Isaiah 2:20-22; Malachi 3:2; Luke 21:36; Revelation 6:15-16; 20:11)

It is very possible that this same hatred of the light that causes the sinner's present self-condemnation will also bring about their self-condemnation in the next life. Although this is horrific, in light of this *self*-condemnation, we cannot easily charge God with injustice. Instead, *it is we who are unjust!* From this perspective, *the sinner is choosing his own destiny*—the darkness in which he feels the greatest sense of comfort. How can this be unjust?

But doesn't this theory circumvent the Bible's teachings that "...we must all appear before the judgment seat of Christ, that each one may receive what is due him for the things done while in the body, whether good or bad" (2 Corinthians 5:10)? Not at all. The great judgment might simply represent an affirmation—a rubber-stamping—*of that which each one of us has already chosen.*

For the children of God, the great judgment will be a time of rejoicing. This is because our fate has already been settled. It is then that we will be changed, "...in a twinkling of an eye" (1 Corinthians 15:50-52) to become like Him (1 John 3:2; 1 Thessalonians 4:14-17). Therefore, when we stand before Him, there will be no doubt about our eternal fate.

It seems that the lover-of-darkness has also sealed his own fate—by running from the light. In view of this possibility, no one can coherently blame God or impugn His righteous, just nature.

Even if hell is self-chosen, isn't God still morally responsible for giving us this choice? Not necessarily. Perhaps God will give the sufferers the option of pulling-the-plug and facing utter annihilation. Even though this option is horrific, it cannot be unjust. If God is the giver of life, there is nothing unjust about allowing the self-condemned to extinguish it.

This is just a possibility. There is nothing in the Scriptures that lays out this option. However, there is nothing that precludes it. Admittedly, there is much about eternal judgment that remains unspecified in the Scriptures.

Can the skeptic coherently say that eternal punishment is unjust? To claim that something is unjust, we need to compare it with an objective standard of justice. However, skeptics have rejected an objective standard in favor of moral relativism. They have become like the math teacher grading an exam without an objectively correct answer key. To try to do so is absurd. Yet, this is exactly what the skeptic does when he claims that eternal punishment is unjust.

When C.S. Lewis was still an atheist, he came to see this very predicament:

- My argument against God was that the universe seemed so cruel and unjust. But how had I got this idea of "just" and "unjust"?...What was I comparing this universe with when I called it unjust?...Of course I could have given up my idea of justice by saying it was nothing but a private idea of my own. But if I did that, then my argument against God collapsed too—for the argument depended on saying that the world was really [objectively] unjust, not simply that it did not happen to please my private fancies…Consequently atheism turns out to be too simple.[3]

Lewis perceived that atheism was unable to bear the weight of his life or to provide the roadmap he needed for navigating it.

The poet and atheist, W.H. Auden, learned the same lesson—that secular humanism is unable to provide any moral basis for our indignation against evil. Auden moved to Brooklyn from his native England in 1939. While he was watching a news clip in a movie theater about the Nazi invasion of Poland, he was horrified to see the audience rise to its feet to applaud and cry out, "Destroy the Poles." Auden wanted to take a strong moral stance against their response, but he realized that—as an atheist—his values were merely self-constructed and, therefore, lacking in any persuasive value. This realization sent him into a moral tailspin, resulting in his becoming a Christian.[4]

Likewise, does any skeptic have a substantive, objective basis for his indignation against the prospect of eternal judgment? Seemingly not.

❖ ❖ ❖

Rather than being unjust, it seems that eternal punishment is a necessary element of justice. Contrary to secular opinion, we need to know that God will ultimately judge. It is this knowledge that enables us to leave aside any thoughts of revenge, hatred, or unforgiveness. Instead, we are free to apply ourselves to that for which we have been called—to love.

Miroslav Volf, who survived the civil wars of the former Yugoslavia, has written:

- The only means of prohibiting all recourses to violence by ourselves is to insist that violence is legitimate only when it comes from God...My thesis is that the practice of non-violence requires a belief in divine vengeance.[5]

Volf knew that his stance would be unpopular in the West. He understood that when we have no substantive experience with being victimized, we also will have no experience of the overwhelming, life-controlling need to avenge.

Writer and theologian Timothy Keller explains:

- Can our passion for justice be honored in a way that does not nurture our desire for blood and vengeance? Volf says the best resource for this is a belief in the concept of God's divine justice. If I don't believe that there is a God who will eventually put all things right, I will take up the sword and will be sucked into the endless vortex of retaliation. Only if I am sure that there's a God who will right all wrongs and settle all accounts perfectly do I have the power to refrain.[6]

However, would the belief in eternal punishment, justice, and hell lead to a more hellish and heartless society? Rather, it seems that the absence of a belief in eternal punishment and justice would push us to seek our own revenge and to pursue our own "justice." Keller observes that in societies where the doctrine of eternal judgment is rejected, brutality reigns:

- Many people complain that belief in a God of judgment will lead to a more brutal society...[but] in both Nazism and Communism...a loss of belief in a God of judgment can lead to brutality. If we are free to shape life and morals any way we choose without ultimate accountability, it can lead to violence. Volf and [poet Czeslaw] Milosz argue that the doctrine of God's final judgment is a necessary undergirding for human practices of love and peacemaking.[7]

PREMISE #2: The God of the Bible promises eternal punishment.

This is true. There are many verses that promise eternal judgment or condemnation. For example:

- "Then they will go away to eternal punishment, but the righteous to eternal life." (Matthew 25:46)

The "eternal punishment" mentioned by Christ in this verse will be just as eternal as the "eternal life" that He conversely mentions. It is understandable that such verses are troubling. However, as we have already pointed out, we do not know the exact nature of this eternal judgment. Once again, perhaps God will offer the sufferer the option of "pulling-the-plug" and thus succumbing to utter annihilation. In light of this uncertainty, the lover-of-light should give God the benefit of the doubt. Therefore, I often respond to these challenges this way:

- I don't know how it will all come out in the end, but I do know that our God is both merciful and just. I also believe that our Creator has the right to judge His creation. If we find this troubling, we should reconcile with Him before it is too late.

CONCLUSION: The God of the Bible cannot be just...or even exist.

Job had also charged God with injustice, and it seemed that he had good reason to do so. God had allowed Satan to deprive him of almost everything, and Job was left devastated. However, his losses did not justify Job's allegations against God.

- Then the LORD answered Job out of the storm. He said: "Who is this that darkens my counsel with words without knowledge? Brace yourself like a man; I will question you, and you shall answer me." (Job 38:1-3)

Chapter 17

The Lord then asked Job a series of questions, and Job could not answer any of them. Job got the point. He understood too little to bring any indictment against God and, therefore, repented:

- The LORD said to Job: "Will the one who contends with the Almighty correct him? Let him who accuses God answer him!" Then Job answered the LORD: "I am unworthy—how can I reply to you? I put my hand over my mouth." (Job 40:1-4)

What made Job unworthy? He was beginning to understand that he had spoken presumptuously about things he did not understand:

- "You [God] asked, 'Who is this that obscures my counsel without knowledge?' Surely I spoke of things I did not understand, things too wonderful for me to know. You [God] said, 'Listen now, and I will speak; I will question you, and you shall answer me.' My ears had heard of you but now my eyes have seen you. Therefore I despise myself and repent in dust and ashes." (Job 42:3-6)

Many will find Job's response repugnant, but why? We too speak about things we do not understand. Although we—humankind—know that we are just a speck in this grand universe, we sometimes act as if we were omniscient. Yet, we cannot even define the basics, like the nature of time, space, matter, or light. The simplest things are beyond our knowing, and yet—like Job—we have the hubris to accuse God of injustice. Perhaps we too need to learn a little humility in keeping with our cosmic insignificance.

If eternal punishment is a reality, then love requires us to warn those around us. The greater the threat, the more genuine must be our drive to warn. This is especially true in regards to eternal punishment. In the West, we glibly dismiss this threat as so barbaric that it couldn't possibly be the design of a God of love. However, like Job, there are times when we refuse to consider how little we truly understand.

Chapter 17

Keller calls hell…

- …simply one's chosen identity apart from God on a trajectory into infinity.[8]

In other words, hell is something we choose. Lewis calls hell…

- …the greatest monument to human freedom.[9]

Keller quotes Lewis' words from *The Great Divorce* as he paints a vivid picture of how we choose hell:

- Hell begins with a grumbling mood, always complaining, always blaming others…but you are still distinct from it. You may even criticize it in yourself and wish you could stop it. But there may come a day when you can no longer. Then there will be no you left to criticize the mood or even to enjoy it, but just the grumble itself, going on forever like a machine. It is not a question of God "sending us" to hell. In each of us there is something growing, which will be hell unless it is nipped in the bud.[10]

How do we nip it? By confessing our sins (1 John 1:9) and crying out for Christ's mercy (Romans 10:12-13). How did we get into this mess? According to Lewis, we continue to harden our heart against the Lord until we have no heart left (Romans 1:24-28). With every refusal to turn away from our sins and turn to Christ, we embrace our final destination. Lewis therefore concludes:

- There are only two kinds of people—those who say "Thy will be done" to God or those to whom God in the end says, "Thy will be done." All that are in Hell choose it.[11]

Is this assessment Biblical? Keller correctly reflects that there are no Biblical accounts of people pleading to be released from hell into God's presence (Luke 16). This makes perfect Scriptural sense. If we hate the light so much in this life that we flee from it, we will flee all the more urgently when confronted with His even greater intensity in the next life (John 3:19-21).

The Apostle Paul taught that we are a stench to those who are perishing (2 Corinthians 2:14-16). How much more will our Lord's glorious presence nauseate those same people in the next life? By that time, their fate will be sealed.

This is horrific. If we love the Lord, what then must we do about those who are bound for hell? We must warn!

MATHEMATICAL VERITIES ARE MIND-DEPENDENT

CHAPTER SUMMARY

Consider the number 1 for a moment. What exactly is it? It is a concept, an idea. We don't find the number 1—or any other number—in nature, apart from our conceptualizations of it. Unlike the rain—which does not depend on what we think about it—the truths of mathematics are mind-dependent.

If this is true about the number 1, it is also true about the numbers 2, 3, 4…And it must also be true about higher level mathematical constructs, like the Pythagorean Theorem:

- $a^2 + b^2 = c^2$

Through this construct, we are always able to determine the length of the longest side of a right-angle triangle by squaring the two other sides, adding this figure and then determining its square root. Amazingly, this answer is exactly what we find when we actually measure a right-angle triangle. Although this mathematical principle is distinct from the material world, it seems to understand the material world, showing us so much about it.

Here is another example: The angles of every triangle contain exactly and invariably, 180 degrees. If you were to add a fourth line or side to the triangle, this four-sided figure would contain angles equaling 180 + 180 = 360 degrees. If you would add a fifth line or side to this four-sided figure, it would contain angles equaling 180 + 360 = 540 degrees, *ad infinitum.*

But from where does this precise symmetry arise? From the consistent relationship between math and the physical world. But what is it that provides such a harmony between those two spheres? These questions speak to the larger question of design, intelligent Design. If the knowledge about our world and the universe is one consistent and harmonious whole, then its source must also be one—the Mind of God—rather than the unconnected, discordant, ever-changing thoughts and contributions of mere men and women.

Clearly, we humans did not create these elegant, precise, and unifying theorems and principles. Instead, *we discovered them*, just as we have discovered so many other marvelous truths about the world! Once again, although distinct from the material world, mathematics seems to understand the material world. Through our knowledge of math, we are told so much about the way things work that it seems like mathematics has an intimate knowledge of the world. By the use of mathematical principles, we have been able to discover aspects of the physical world even before we have observed them "in nature," so-to-speak. How can we account for this amazing correspondence? Design...intelligent Design!

If mathematics is conceptual and, therefore, mind-dependent—and yet does not depend upon our minds—then there must be a universal and immutable Mind that it does depend upon.

To state this another way:

> PREMISE #1: Mathematical truths are conceptual and therefore require the involvement of a mind.

> PREMISE #2: Our human minds are not adequate or proficient enough to account for the uniformity, immutability, and elegance that we find in mathematical realities.

> CONCLUSION: Therefore, a greater, immutable Mind must exist.

Chapter 19

BERTRAND RUSSELL AND THE NATURAL LAW PROOF

CHAPTER SUMMARY

The mathematician Bertrand Russell was awarded the Nobel Prize for Literature in 1950. As an atheist, he wrote against various theistic proofs. One of them was the proof from natural law, which states that the natural laws require a law-giver.

Bertrand Russell failed to engage the genuine theistic argument. Instead, he chose to cite an example of a "natural law" which no apologist would ever cite:

- There is, as we all know, a law that if you throw dice you will get double sixes only about once in thirty-six times, and we do not regard that as evidence that the fall of the dice is regulated by design; on the contrary, if the double sixes came every time we should think that there was design.[1]

This is not a "natural law," but a logical law of chance and probability. No one would claim that "the fall of the dice is regulated by design," unless he or she was trying to argue that chance is a matter of design. However, no ID—intelligent Design—proponent would ever try to do that.

Russell then obfuscated:

- ...but natural laws are a description of how things do in fact behave, and being a mere description of what they in fact do, you cannot argue that there must be somebody who told them to do that, because even supposing that there were, you are then faced with the question, "Why did God issue just those natural laws and no others?"[2]

Of course the natural laws describe "how things do...behave," but they are more than a mere description. They also invoke causal agents. These agents or laws are elegant and immutable, certainly not the products of chance, or of explosions.

Russell then asked an irrelevant question about why God issued just those natural laws and no others. He assumed that if we—the proponents of ID—could not answer this question, our theory must be wrong.

Let's apply this same standard to Russell and ask: "What are time, space, light, and matter?" No one can answer these questions definitively. However, because there are no adequate answers to these questions, should we dismiss the entire body of scientific knowledge? Certainly not! Then likewise, we should not dismiss the proof of God from the laws of science simply because we cannot answer every question. If knowledge in science, theology, or any other field of study required complete knowledge of the subject, we would all be reduced to silence.

❖   ❖   ❖

Russell never engages the heart of the "natural law" argument. A law-giver is necessary in order to account for:

> ✓ the immutability of the natural laws in a universe of molecules-in-motion;

> ✓ the elegance of the natural laws, which reveals incredible design;

> ✓ the precise fine-tuning of the universe;

> ✓ the origin of the natural laws even before anything natural had yet been brought into existence;

> ✓ the universal and uniform impact of the natural laws throughout the universe. The effect of these laws is not localized, as are radio waves. This suggests that the natural laws emanate from the Transcendent.

Chapter 19

All of these proofs were irrelevant to Russell and remain so to the atheists of our day. They claim that the wide variety of theistic proofs have all been refuted. In actuality, the findings of science have revived them.

PART II
THE FRUITS OF CHRISTIANITY

AN INTRODUCTION TO PART II:
THE FRUITS OF CHRISTIANITY

CHAPTER SUMMARY
Instead of attempting to prove the existence of God, the chapters in Part II will try to prove the reality of the Christian God by pointing to the evidence of His promised blessings.

Jesus declared:

- "...every healthy tree bears good fruit, but the diseased tree bears bad fruit. A healthy tree cannot bear bad fruit, nor can a diseased tree bear good fruit. Every tree that does not bear good fruit is cut down and thrown into the fire. Thus you will recognize them by their fruits." (Matthew 7:17-20)

While Jesus was applying this analogy to the question of recognizing false teachers, it also applies to recognizing false religions. Consequently, one indication of the truth is found in the fruit that it bears. The Apostle James taught that we can use this reasoning to identify the wisdom that comes from the Lord. It will bear good fruit:

- ...let him show his works in the meekness of wisdom. But if you have bitter jealousy and selfish ambition in your hearts, do not boast and be false to the truth. This is not the wisdom that comes down from above, but is earthly, unspiritual, demonic. For where jealousy and selfish ambition exist, there will be disorder and every vile practice. But the wisdom from above is first pure, then peaceable, gentle, open to reason, full of mercy and good fruits, impartial and sincere. (James 3:13-17)

As clouds produce rain, Godly wisdom produces a harvest. In these final chapters, I want to demonstrate that the wisdom of the Bible produces a goodly harvest. This is the very thing that the *Book of Proverbs* informs us will happen when we follow God:

- ...wisdom will come into your heart, and knowledge will be pleasant to your soul; discretion will watch over you, understanding will guard you, delivering you from the way of evil...(Proverbs 2:10-12)

If the Christian faith displays and proves the truth of this uncommon wisdom—found in a Book that is 2000 years old—we must also ask about the uncommon Source of such wisdom.

EXCEPTIONS TO THE RULE

This introduction, with its promise of benefits for the Christian, does not pertain to those who have not sanctified the Lord in their heart (1 Peter 3:15). Neither does it pertain to those who have not made Him their first concern (Matthew 6:33). Nor does it always pertain to a relatively new Christian.

For a number of years as a believer, I suffered unimaginably. I had carried a lot of counter-biblical beliefs into my life with Christ. These attitudes and perspectives had to be burned away; my cup had to be emptied before I could be filled and enabled to live for Christ. I had to learn that being humbled was a prerequisite for being blessed (Hebrews 12:5-11). Now, I can say along with the Psalmist:

- It is good for me that I was afflicted, that I might learn your statutes. The law of your mouth is better to me than thousands of gold and silver pieces. (Psalm 119:71-72)

Nevertheless, I continue to endure afflictions to this day. We are warned in Scripture that if we want to live for Jesus, we will also have to suffer like Jesus. Therefore, along with the blessings will come the sufferings:

Chapter 20

- [We are]...persecuted, but not forsaken; struck down, but not destroyed; always carrying in the body the death of Jesus, so that the life of Jesus may also be manifested in our bodies. For we who live are always being given over to death for Jesus' sake, so that the life of Jesus also may be manifested in our mortal flesh. (2 Corinthians 4:9-11)

As humbling must precede being lifted up, suffering must precede blessing. The glass must be emptied before it can be filled. And all of this occurs in an on-going process that takes place throughout the course of our lives. However, in most of the next chapters, the focus will be on the filling.

Chapter 21

THE "DEATH" OF GOD AND HOW IT HAS CHANGED THE WORLD

CHAPTER SUMMARY

When we reject God, we also reject the essential values of civilization and human thriving.

The German philosopher, Friedrich Nietzsche, declared that once a society and culture rejects the Christian God, they are also rejecting and denying the validity of Christian values—concepts like equality, human exceptionalism, and an entire array of associated ethics and standards. However, the West naively thinks that it is possible to retain and utilize those same values even after "killing" the Christian God and declaring any belief in Him to be totally groundless and illogical. Os Guinness wrote of Nietzsche's disdain for such blindness:

- Nietzsche was a self-proclaimed "anti-Christ," yet he had no time for complacent middle-class thinking that could say, "God is dead" and go on living as before. If God was "dead" for Western culture, then nothing was the same. It was time to face the consequences.[1]

What were the consequences? Primarily, anything would now be permissible. With God in the grave, our only moral rudder would be our desires, our fears, and our prejudices. In fact, it wouldn't be too much of a stretch to say that the collateral damage of the death of God included the two world wars of the 20th century.

However, as in Nietzsche's day, so too in ours. Few among us can fully perceive the horrific consequences of their rejection of God. Yet atheists confidently explain:

- Once anyone rejects God, there is no need to sink into a morally relativistic quagmire. After all, we still have absolute moral principles to guide us. Here is just one of many

151

examples: Drinking water is absolutely good. It promotes survival, and survival is absolutely good.

However, what is it about survival that makes it absolutely good? Is there any way that we can establish that survival is good, apart from our own subjective judgment? Taking this another step further, if there are no absolute principles to guide us, how can we say that human survival is any more important than the survival of a mosquito? If the mosquito could talk, he might say that his survival is just as important to him as ours is to us. Who could say anything against that sort of logic with any authority, if God is dead? Is there anything left to argue in favor of laws that protect us over the denizens of the insect world, other than human chauvinism? There is a growing number of people who would now proclaim proudly, "No!"

This brings us back to the idea of moral relativism, where morality is entirely relative to how one thinks and feels on any given morning. In *Twilight of the Idols*, Nietzsche wrote:

- They are rid of the Christian God and now believe all the more firmly that they must cling to the Christian morality...When one gives up the Christian faith, one pulls the right to Christian morality out from under one's feet.[2]

Truly, Christian morality rests upon an absolutely immutable and universal standard—God. But does that really matter? Yes! Our beliefs have consequences. Without resting on an adequate moral foundation, morality becomes little more than a biochemical reaction, a dusting of snow that melts as soon as the sun appears. The German-Jewish poet-turned-Lutheran, Heinrich Heine, noted the portentous consequences of such a loss of solidly-based morality back in 1832:

- It is to the great merit of Christianity that it has somewhat attenuated the brutal German lust for battle. But it could not destroy it entirely. And should that taming talisman break— the Cross—then will come roaring back the wild madness of the ancient warriors.[3]

What would happen once the authority of the Cross was "broken"? Heine continued:

- And laugh not at my forebodings, the advice of a dreamer who warns you away from the Kants and Fichtes of the world, and from our philosophers of nature. No, laugh not at the visionary who knows that in the realm of phenomena comes soon the revolution that has already taken place in the realm of spirit. For thought goes before deed as lightning before thunder. There will be played in Germany a play compared to which the French revolution was but an innocent idyll.[4]

So, what is the problem with "the Kants and Fichtes of the world"? Perhaps that their philosophies and the "categorical imperatives" they have concocted are insubstantial and powerless to restrain the madness! The late psychiatrist and Holocaust survivor, Victor Frankl, wrote about the reason for, and the origin, of the madness:

- I am absolutely convinced that the gas chambers of Auschwitz, Treblinka, and Maidanek, were ultimately prepared not in some ministry or other in Berlin, but rather at the desks and the lecture halls of nihilistic scientists and philosophers.[5]

Thoughts and philosophies precede plans and actions. Historian Richard Weikart, of California State University, wrote about how the anti-God worldview of Darwinism impacts thought and action:

- By reducing humans to mere animals, by stressing human inequality, and by viewing the death of many "unfit" organisms as a necessary—and even progressive—natural phenomenon, Darwinism made the death of the "inferior" seem inevitable and even beneficent. Some Darwinists concluded that helping the "unfit" die—which had for millennia been called murder—was not morally reprehensible, but was rather morally good.[6]

Hitler did not invent eugenics. Instead, he gladly imbibed ideas that had become ripe in the post-Christian Western world. According to Weikart, Darwinist thinking brought about policy and behavioral change:

- Those skeptical about the role Darwinism played in the rise of advocacy for involuntary euthanasia, infanticide, and abortion should consider several points. First, before the rise of Darwinism, there was no debate on these issues, as there was almost universal agreement in Europe that human life is sacred and that all innocent human lives should be protected. Second, the earliest advocates of involuntary euthanasia, infanticide, and abortion in Germany were devoted to a Darwinian worldview. Third, Haeckel, the most famous Darwinist in Germany, promoted these ideas in some of his best-selling books, so these ideas reached a wide audience, especially among those receptive to Darwinism. Finally, Haeckel and other Darwinists and eugenicists grounded their views on death and killing on their naturalistic interpretation of Darwinism.[7]

Heine was clearly right. In the same way that lightning precedes thunder, thought precedes deed. In *Markings*, the late Secretary General of the United Nations, Dag Hammarskjold, wrote:

- God does not die on the day when we cease to believe in a personal deity, but we die on the day when our loves cease to be illuminated by the steady radiance, renewed daily, of a wonder, the source of which is beyond all reason.[8]

❖ ❖ ❖

After we "kill" God, the resulting death takes many forms. Jesus had taught: "You are of more value than many sparrows." (Matthew 10:31). Up to two hundred years ago, such a statement would not have raised an eyebrow. However, today it has become quite controversial within certain circles, where it is claimed that all life is of equal value.

Chapter 21

Most people still believe that we are more valuable than sparrows, mosquitoes, or even cows. But how do they justify this claim in our post-Christian society? Offering various possibilities, they might say that humanity is more valuable than other forms of life because we are sentient beings. Or, because we feel and love more deeply, or that we are intelligent and creative...or any number of other things.

These criteria, by themselves, are totally inadequate to justify the surpassing value of human life. The question of value simply gets shifted to other baseless markers— intelligence, feelings, or creativity. But once again, how is value imputed to these criteria in a God-less world, which lacks any inherent meaning?

Nietzsche perceived this problem in the late 19th century:

- God is dead. God remains dead. And we have killed him. How shall we comfort ourselves, the murderers of all murderers? What was holiest and mightiest of all that the world has yet owned has bled to death under our knives: who will wipe this blood off us? What water is there for us to clean ourselves? What festivals of atonement, what sacred games shall we have to invent? Is not the greatness of this deed too great for us? Must we ourselves not become gods simply to appear worthy of it?[9]

Nietzsche realized that without God, it would be necessary for us to "become gods." Why would this be so essential? *So that we might subjectively create our own values.* There is no alternative.

However, we encounter a huge problem when we try to create value in a valueless, meaningless universe. The way we determine or assign value cannot match the way that God determines it. For example, if our value depends on our higher intelligence, then we must sacrifice other values—like human equality—in the process.

Why is that? Well, some of us are more intelligent, conscious, sensitive, or educated than others. Furthermore, adults are more intelligent than babies and the elderly. They are also more successful and contribute more to society. This means that equality must find its support beyond any of these metrics. Actually, support for true equality must come from beyond the physical world—from God—as our *Declaration of Independence* declares:

- We hold these truths to be self-evident, that all men are created equal, that they are endowed by their Creator with certain unalienable Rights…

Sadly, these truths are no longer self-evident. Once we reject God and His valuation of us, we must seek our self-definition from our social context. But do we want to live in a world where our relative value is socially determined according to our intelligence, performance, or status? Of course not! Nevertheless, when we reject God, we require a God-replacement to determine our value. We do this on our own, but since we are social creatures, we are susceptible and vulnerable to the tyrannical opinions of others. Therefore, we adopt our value from the words and actions of others and, in the process, become imprisoned to their opinions.

The problems do not stop there. Once we reject the only possible basis for equality, we also reject justice. When some are more valued than others, there is no longer an adequate reason to treat one another as equals, with equal protection before the law.

In fact, when we reject God, we reject any coherent and just system of laws and values. Atheist Arthur Leff of the Duke School of Law had this to say about that:

- The so-called death of God wasn't just His funeral, but was the elimination of any coherent ethical or legal system…As it stands now, everything is up for grabs…Napalming babies is bad, starving the poor wicked, buying and selling people is depraved—but, 'Sez who?' God help us.[10]

Leff understood that, without God, there is no basis for any objective system of values or laws. Instead, we have banished ourselves to a meaningless, valueless, lifeless desert—self-condemned to obsessively and hopelessly try to prove that we have value.

As a result, we now find many competing systems of "justice." For one example, we currently have what is known as "Identity Politics." According to this point of view, justice is no longer about the guilt or innocence of an individual based upon whether or not he or she has committed a crime. Instead, justice is determined by one's membership in a particular class of people—based upon race, sex, color, or sexual orientation. The classes of people identified as oppressed are favored, while those identified as oppressors are denigrated.

Others go so far as to reject any notion of justice. For them, each of us is merely a product of our nurture and our genetic nature. From this point of view, punishment is no longer appropriate on the basis of guilt, since guilt is no longer acceptable. What remains? Just therapy and "love"—the carrot, but no stick!

Without the Christian God and His concept of justice, there remains little for the restraining of our lusts and absolutely nothing for the inspiration of society. If God is dead, then anything good took its last breath as well.

❖ ❖ ❖

Is this a proof for the existence of God? I raise this question because skeptics bring it up when they are forced into a logical corner. They will say: "Prove that your God exists." Generally, they present this challenge, not because they are ready to evaluate the evidence, but because they don't want to lose the argument.

At this point, the most important thing for us to know is that there are many sound reasons to believe that our Savior does exist. Still, we may face times when we begin to doubt our experience and our understanding of God. Even John the Baptist had his doubts about Jesus. In Matthew 11, we read the story about how John sent his disciples to Jesus and asked for confirmatory evidence regarding His Messiah-ship. Jesus did not send the disciples back to John with a message saying, "Just believe!" Instead, He told them to tell John about the evidences they had seen—evidences supporting His identity. We too need evidence to bolster our faith. When we have it, we will be able to struggle successfully with our doubts as we face the many challenges of life:

- …you have been grieved by various trials, so that the tested genuineness of your faith—more precious than gold that perishes though it is tested by fire—may be found to result in praise and glory and honor at the revelation of Jesus Christ. (1 Peter 1:6-7)

DO THE BENEFITS
OF FAITH IN GOD
OFFER ANY EVIDENCE
FOR THE EXISTENCE OF GOD?

CHAPTER SUMMARY

The benefits of believing in Christ are hard to deny. If this faith represented a distortion of reality, the Christian would be paying a tremendous price for believing this "illusion." However, this is not what is happening. Therefore, it seems that this faith provides a light which enables the successful navigation of the real world.

Theistic proofs take many forms. Some of them focus on our experiences. Here is one example: If Christian beliefs enable the Christian to live longer and more joyfully, does this fact say anything about the existence of the Christian God? While the atheist would reject the idea that emotional, psychological, or physical benefits have anything to do with truth, most people would acknowledge this relationship.

According to the deist Ben Franklin, we even need God for a moral society:

- If men are wicked with religion, what would they be without it?[1]

The benefits of the Christian faith even extend to our most intimate relationships, as former atheist, Patrick Glynn, reports:

- A 1978 study found that church attendance predicted marital satisfaction better than any other single variable. Couples in long-lasting marriages who were surveyed in another study listed religion as one of the most important "prescriptions" of a happy marriage.[2]

For most Christians, such observations are as predictable as night following day. We have long seen how the Lord and His wisdom are the saving balm for our relationships. Glynn also shows a correspondence between religious belief and physical and emotional well-being:

- Religious belief is one of the most consistent correlates of overall mental health and happiness. Study after study has shown a powerful relationship between religious belief and practice, on the one hand, and healthy behaviors with regard to such problems as suicide, alcohol and drug abuse, divorce, depression, even, perhaps surprisingly, levels of sexual satisfaction in marriage...[3]

I can also attest heartily to this. Jesus said,

- "If you hold to my teaching, you are really my disciples. Then you will know the truth, and the truth will set you free." (John 8:31-32)

My life in Christ has freed me from my self-delusions. I have been enabled to accept myself and satisfyingly navigate the real world of people and things.

In contrast to this, the experience of the atheist is admittedly dismal, although it might commence with a sense of freedom from guilt and constraints. Jean-Paul Sartre confessed that, "Atheism is a cruel, long-term business."[4] Bertrand Russell described his atheistic faith in this manner:

- The life of man is a long march through the night, surrounded by invisible foes, tortured by weariness and pain...Brief and powerless is man's life; on him and all his race the slow, sure doom falls pitiless and dark. Blind to good and evil, reckless of destruction, omnipotent matter rolls on its relentless way.[5]

H.J. Blackham, a former director of the British Humanist Association, wrote:

- The most drastic objection to humanism is that it is too bad to be true. The world is one vast tomb if humans are ephemeral and human life itself is doomed to ultimate extinction...There is no end to hiding from the ultimate end of life, which is death. But it does not avail. On humanist assumptions, life leads to nothing, and every pretense that it does not is a deceit.[6]

Does any of this offer any objective evidence for the existence of God? I would say so. The things that Christians choose tend to bring objective benefits. This is of course true of the animal world. The creatures of the wild seem to have been endowed with "wisdom." Grazing animals tend to eat nutritious greens while rejecting the plants that are poisonous. They know to drink when they get thirsty, to find shade when they get hot, and to rest when they get tired. They are able to make positive adjustments to an objective reality that surrounds them, and they derive benefits from this.

Conversely, delusion is strongly associated with heavy costs, and not benefits. If we are deluded or simply mistaken about which roads to take to get to our destination, our trip will be more costly. Why then, if Christians are deluded about God, do they derive unmistakable benefits from their "delusion"? Instead, it would seem that Christians are doing something right, even wise and in-touch with a reality that eludes others.

Is it possible to flourish through distorted thinking? Atheists claim that religious belief is a matter of gross self-delusion. They have many pejorative phrases to describe faith in God: "imaginary friend," "big-daddy in the sky," "self-delusion," or even "complete nonsense."

However, these charges do not seem to be consistent with the reality of Christian lives and societies. Our delusions should put us out-of-touch with reality, especially the supposed "God delusion" that lies at the foundation of our entire lives as Christians. Instead of assisting us to constructively manage our jobs, our relationships, our home lives and daily activities—all of which require accurate feedback—delusions about a God should interfere with any positive adjustments we might make. Instead, we flourish, even in the midst of hardships.

How can this be? Think about riding your bicycle blindfolded. You would soon crash, incurring great costs. Closer to home, consider someone who navigates life with rose-colored glasses. He might think that all women secretly love him, and this gives him a high, at least in the short run. As a consequence, he doesn't take "no" for an answer. I knew such a man who was arrested repeatedly for "harassment" because of this cognitive distortion. Because of his delusion, he just wouldn't take "no" as an answer.

Cognitive distortions inevitably incur a cost. Consider a woman who was confident that she was performing better on the job than she really was. As a result, she saw no need for improvement and was eventually fired.

Or, consider people who are deluded into thinking that they are treating others caringly when, in fact, they really aren't. Eventually, they lose their friends.

Generally speaking, distorted thinking has its costs. In her book *It's All in the Playing*, Shirley MacLaine confidently explained her distorted faith:

- I went on to express my feeling of total responsibility and power for all events that occur in the world because the world is happening only in my reality. And human beings feeling pain, terror, depression, panic, and so forth, were really only aspects of pain, terror, depression, panic, and so on, in me![7]

How would such distorted thinking affect her relationships, or the way she views the world? Wikipedia concluded its posting on MacLaine in this way:

- In 2015, she sparked criticism for her comments on Jews, Christians, and Stephen Hawking. In particular she claimed that victims of the Nazi Holocaust were experiencing the results of their own karma, and suggested that Hawking subconsciously caused himself to develop ALS as a means to focus better on physics.[8]

Understandably, Shirley MacLaine's thinking created relational problems, among other things. Why then do those who believe in a "heavenly Christian daddy-in-the-sky"—an all-encompassing "delusion"—make positive adjustments, while others do not?

Perhaps Christians are on to something real. But how? Through believing in the words on the pages of a Book written two thousand years ago? How could honoring and following our Bible enable us to successfully navigate life?

I hope that the next few chapters will demonstrate how the wisdom and practices found in our ancient Book have led to positive changes, even on a global level.

Chapter 23

A PHILOSOPHY OF SUFFERING

CHAPTER SUMMARY

Suffering is part of life, and so we need a worldview that helps us to make the most of it. It is the Biblical worldview that enables us to endure it.

The late British philosopher C.S. Lewis declared that he believed in Christianity for the same reason he believed in the sun. It was not merely because he could see the sun, but, by the sun, *he could see everything else.*[1]

By the light of the Bible, are we enabled to see and understand everything else?

- The natural person does not accept the things of the Spirit of God, for they are folly to him, and he is not able to understand them because they are spiritually discerned. The spiritual person judges all things, but is himself to be judged by no one. "For who has understood the mind of the Lord so as to instruct him?" But we have the mind of Christ. (1 Corinthians 2:14-16)

Both Scripture and experience have proven to me that, through His Word, Jesus has given us the eyes to see. I will confine myself to two instances of this principle—what the Bible has to say about suffering, and what the Bible has to say about sin.

The Bible enables us to understand and embrace suffering and to live meaningfully within its inevitable grip. In contrast to this, secularism regards suffering as a useless encumbrance. Consequently, when the secularist suffers, he experiences a double whammy—a virtual knockout punch:

1. The suffering itself and…
2. …the debilitating belief that suffering is a negative, meaningless and costly burden, lacking any redemptive value.

Secularism deprives suffering of its meaning, but that doesn't mean that secularists don't talk about meaning. The philosopher Friedrich Nietzsche had this to say:

- He who has a why to live for can bear almost any how.[2]

Although this is very true, it is not adequate to simply *create* our own "why." We need to know that *meaning is intrinsic to reality itself*...that it connects us to something higher than our changing feelings.

The late American novelist Norman Mailer was cognizant of this problem:

- We are healthier if we think there is some importance in what we're doing...When it seems like my life is meaningless, I feel closer to despair.[3]

Mailer realized that he could not merely create his own meaning. Instead, *meaning must be discovered within the fabric of objective reality*. Consequently, inventing meaning is no more meaningful than imagining that we have a wife and children—a family—when we do not. Imagination might fill our emptiness for a while, but eventually there will be a price that must be paid.

Without assurance of real meaning, we shrivel and die in the face of suffering. During his internment in a National Socialist death camp, the late psychiatrist Viktor Frankl observed:

- The prisoner who had lost faith in the future...was doomed.[4]

Even worse, according to sociologist David Karp, secularism slams the door on meaning:

- Cosmopolitan medicine banishes that knowledge [of the necessary purpose for suffering] by insisting that suffering is without meaning, and unnecessary... [Sufferings are] secularized as mechanical mishaps...[5]

Nevertheless, secularists do find meaning in suffering. They recognize that suffering can aid in producing character and virtue. However, are these observations enough to redeem the pain of suffering, disease, victimization, or death? Hardly. For one who has lost his family to a murderer, it would be of little comfort to acknowledge that, during his brief sojourn through life, his ordeal might be improving his character.

Confidence in the meaning of suffering and of life itself is essential. It is precisely this meaning that the Bible enables us to see and embrace.

We trust in the Bible's wisdom that, in order to become like Christ, we must suffer like Christ (2 Corinthians 4:10-11, 16-18). Besides, knowing that our suffering has a purpose and will last for only a little while can help us to persevere. This perspective helped our Lord, as well:

- Looking to Jesus, the founder and perfecter of our faith, who for the joy that was set before him endured the cross, despising the shame, and is seated at the right hand of the throne of God. (Hebrews 12:2, ESV)

We need a worldview that serves as a good roadmap, getting us to where we need to go. The Bible's teachings on suffering enable us to navigate even the most horrendous roads.

However, there are some aberrant forms of Christianity that rob us of this confidence. Their proponents claim that we have the power in our tongues to create the world as we would like it to be, thus delivering us from the grip of suffering. Subsequently, when suffering does not relent, and the tongue has proven unable to deliver them, they are blindsided by this failure. A sense of spiritual inadequacy and confusion can be the residue of such wrong-headed thinking.

Chapter 23

A PHILOSOPHY OF VIGILANCE

I was never able to put two and two together and recognize the negative effects of sugar until it was pointed out to me. Since that time, I have become more and more aware of how sugar makes me feel. I now limit my intake.

Similarly the Spirit, through the wisdom and knowledge found in the Bible, has made me aware of both the evil of sin...and of the destructive impact it has upon me. I began to see the deception of sin—how it coerces me to justify and even defend it. If I allow it, sin takes control of my thinking in a more profound way than any drug ever could. Now, with my eyes opened wide by the teachings of Scripture, I can begin to oppose it and not fall prey to its corrupting influence.

The Scriptures have unmasked within me deep sins, like jealousy. I was jealous of the joy that other Christians were experiencing in the Lord. I therefore sought to undermine their confidence by finding flaws in their faith and in their understanding of Scripture. What I was doing was pure evil, but I had been blinded. When the Holy Spirit began to reveal these things through Scripture, I was horrified. I tried to rationalize my sin. Fortunately for me, it became increasingly difficult to deny what I was doing. I was crushed, but I found comfort in the Lord when I confessed my sins.

Admittedly, I still struggle against sin daily. However, now I can see *immediately* its ugly influence. When it begins to take hold, I confess it to my Savior; He forgives and cleanses me of all of its filth (1 John 1:9). Then He gives me the confidence to once again assault sin's fortifications.

Sin is a cancer. Without the confidence of God's forgiveness and intimate involvement in our lives, we will inevitably condemn ourselves by covering over our sins...instead of bringing them into the light. But they are still there, festering freely in the darkness, wrapping their cancerous tentacles around everything in us and all our intentions. We may do amazing things—giving generously to the poor, building hospitals, volunteering our services and obtaining advanced degrees. But the sin is still there, calling out its commands at the very helm of our ship.

The Bible is our map and navigational instrument. Without it, we will inevitably end up shipwrecked, on unforeseen rocks. *Proverbs* states that God's wisdom is essential for our navigation through life:

- Blessed is the one who finds wisdom, and the one who gets understanding, for the gain from her is better than gain from silver and her profit better than gold. She is more precious than jewels, and nothing you desire can compare with her. Long life is in her right hand; in her left hand are riches and honor. Her ways are ways of pleasantness, and all her paths are peace. She is a tree of life to those who lay hold of her; those who hold her fast are called blessed. (Proverbs 3:13-18)

How does all of this prove that God exists? If the Bible—written from 3,500 to 2,000 years ago—can provide such a reliable roadmap and guide for healthy living, it suggests that its mostly poorly-educated writers must have been inspired from Above. Furthermore, we who are in Christ are being enlightened every day by the Holy Spirit so that we might understand its truths (1 Corinthians 2:12-14).

In the next chapter, I will try to illustrate how the teaching of the Bible is the best way for us to address the issues of mental health and the wise management of our lives.

Chapter 24

THE BIBLE AND DEPRESSION
(This essay was originally published in the
Christian Research Journal.)

CHAPTER SUMMARY
The Bible offers the ultimate counsel in dealing with depression and other forms of despair. This points to its divine origin.

In many ways, the Bible embodies evidence that it is the product of a superior Intelligence. This can be demonstrated by examining Biblical wisdom regarding human psychology, especially when we compare it to the secular solutions that are offered for psychological and emotional well-being.

THANKFULNESS AND DEPRESSION

Thankfulness is great for body and soul and even for depression. According to Lauren Aaronson:

- Feeling thankful and expressing that thanks makes you happier and heartier...Just jot down things that make you thankful...Call it corny, but gratitude just may be the glue that holds society together.[1]

In other words, "Just do it!" Although helpful, thankfulness without God and an assurance of heaven can be irrational and delusional. Just consider someone who is terminally ill, has lost family and friends, and has nothing tangible to look forward to but death. Besides being insensitive, advising her to be thankful is asking her to be irrational. Although thankfulness might work emotionally, it would require this client to lobotomize her mind and *deny* the most significant aspects of her life.

In addition to this, there remains the awkward question: "Thankful to whom?" Yes, thankfulness makes sound psychological sense, but Aaronson avoids this obvious question. It's like throwing a party without inviting the host!

Thankfulness demands that we open our eyes and acknowledge that there must be some entity that should be acknowledged. This all comes very naturally and comfortably for the Christian, who has no need to make believe that the Host doesn't exist. In fact, the Host is the lynchpin tying it all neatly together, making sense out of thankless situations. Asaph, the Psalmist, writes: "My flesh and my heart may fail, but God is the strength of my heart and my portion forever" (Psalm 73:26, NIV). Besides, practicing Biblical thankfulness does not require those who are depressed to deny the painful realities of their lives.

HOPE AND DEPRESSION

Depressed people need hope more than anything else. They have been fighting a foe that is greater than they are, and they have despaired of their own efforts. Psychiatrist and Holocaust survivor Viktor Frankl observed many fellow prisoners struggle and finally acquiesce to the verdict of the death camps. In *The Journey: Our Quest for Faith and Meaning,* Os Guiness quotes Frankl:

- The prisoner who had lost his faith in the future—his future—was doomed. With his loss of belief in the future, he also lost his spiritual hold; he let himself decline and become subject to mental and physical decay.[2]

Frankl understood that the best elixir for despair is hope. The Bible concurs: "A man's spirit sustains him in sickness, but a crushed spirit who can bear?" (Proverbs 8:14). But how does one obtain the hope that sustains? In *The Noonday Demon*, coined by one reviewer as "the definitive book on depression," Andrew Solomon—himself a long-time sufferer—writes:

- Since depression is highly demotivating, it takes a certain survivor impulse to keep going through the depression, not to cave into it. A sense of humor is the best indicator that you will recover; it is often the best indicator that people will love you. Sustain that and you have hope.[3]

A sense of humor is a great gift. Some have a natural endowment, while others have to learn it. However, it's more than a skill—it's also a vision of life. One who has this skill can laugh in the midst of his foibles...*precisely because they are mere foibles.* This is especially true when our foibles are seen in the light of eternity (Romans 8:18-19), and not in the actual substance of daily life. Andrew Solomon understood the difficulty of laughter in the context of his reality:

- Of course it can be hard to sustain a sense of humor during an experience that is really not so funny. It is urgently necessary to do so...Whatever time is eaten by a depression is gone forever. The minutes that are ticking by as you experience the illness are minutes that you will not know again. No matter how bad you feel you have to do everything you can to keep living, even if all you can do for the moment is breathe. Wait it out and occupy the time of waiting as fully as you can. That's my big piece of advice to depressed people.[4]

Do better...try harder! That's not very hopeful—especially not for those who really need hope. Indeed, all of us must often wait for hope to re-emerge, but we also need to know that, when we are at our weakest and lowest, we are actually at our highest, according to 2 Corinthians 12:9-10. We need the assurance that even in the midst of depression, our dear Lord is drawing near to us in our pain (Isaiah 57:15; 66:1-2; Psalm 34:17-18), is suffering along with us (Hebrews 4:15; Isaiah 63:7-11), and is working even our defeats and failures towards a blessed and eternal conclusion (Romans 8:28; Philippians 1:6; John 6:37-40).

Psychiatrist M. Scott Peck, author of *The Road Less Traveled*, wrote about his journey from Zen Buddhism to Christianity. He had repeatedly observed that his Christian clients would improve, no matter how serious their psychiatric condition. He concluded:

- The quickest way to change your attitude toward pain is to accept the fact that everything that happens to us has been designed for our spiritual growth...We cannot lose once we realize that everything that happens to us has been designed to teach us holiness…We are guaranteed winners![5]

Peck's words ring true. But if our hope is in ourselves rather than in our omnipotent and all-loving God, we have no guarantees except death and decay. Returning to the words of Andrew Solomon once again, he also expressed his appreciation for the power of "faith":

- Frankly, I think that the best treatment for depression is belief, which is in itself far more essential than what you believe in. If you really truly believe that you can relieve your depression by standing on your head and spitting nickels for an hour every afternoon, it is likely that this incommodious activity will do you tremendous good.[6]

Indeed, it is a well-demonstrated fact that the placebo effect is powerful. If we believe in something—anything—it will make a difference, at least in the short-run. However, unless our faith accords with reality—our experiences and observations—and is nurtured by compelling evidences…it will evaporate, and along with it, any positive influence.

God has not left His suffering people destitute of many compelling reasons for hope. He has not been slack in providing authenticating miracles—Matthew 11:5-6; John 5:31-36; 10:37; 20:25-31; Acts 1:3; Hebrews 2:4. In addition, He has also provided many instances of fulfilled prophecy to reassure our fretful minds—Luke 24:25-27, 44-45; John 14:28-29; 16:1-4, 32-33; Acts 17:2-4; 18:4; 28:23.

The alternative to a trust in God is a trust in self. Such a self-trust is constantly under attack by our experiences, which tend to indict this notion. We know we're not worthy of self-trust and, consequently, this trust in ourselves can be maintained only through a most repressive form of denial. Nevertheless, we yearn to trust. However, trust can only flourish fully when we are finally married to our intended, ideal Husband.

Chapter 24

AUTHENTICITY,
SELF-ACCEPTANCE AND DEPRESSION

We need to be authentic and at peace with our true self, but this is difficult. When we lack authenticity and transparency, we are in a state of disharmony and conflict. We obsess about maintaining an image, a lie. Karen Wright offers this:

- Authenticity is correlated with many aspects of psychological well-being, including vitality, self-esteem, and coping skills. Acting in accordance with one's core self—a trait called self-determination—is ranked by some experts as one of the three basic psychological needs.[7]

Here are some of Wright's suggestions for achieving authenticity: reading novels, meditating, cultivating solitude, and playing hard. These suggest that all we need to do is spend some quality time with ourselves. She also maintains that we should "be willing to lose" and cites Thomas Moore's rationale:

- Feelings of inauthenticity are heightened by a lack of a philosophy that allows failure to be part of life. If you're leading a full life, you are going to fail some every day.[8]

Moore is correct—failure is a part of life. We need to learn to graciously accept that fact, rather than deny our failures. Such a denial would be totally inauthentic. However, finding a philosophy that supports that kind of perspective is not easy. Secularism can't provide it. If you believe that this life is all we have, then failure assumes monumental importance. Thus, because of our limited time, secularism places an even greater burden to succeed on our shoulders. If we fail to achieve, well, it seems as if there is no mercy for those who stumble.

Buddhism is more compassionate and accepting of failure, but this empathy comes at a great price. It diminishes the significance of failure because failure is illusion. But then again, so too is the rest of life. Life in this temporal world of illusion must be transcended through enlightenment. However, "enlightenment" is a matter of recognizing that everything we value—friends, family, vocation, beauty—is *also* illusion. Buddhism therefore represents a denial, not just of failure, but of everything.

Authenticity and self-acceptance are rare commodities. Psychologist Shelley E. Taylor sums up the clinical evidence:

- People are positively biased in their assessments of themselves and of their ability to control what goes on around them, as well as in their views of the future. The widespread existence of these biases and the ease with which they can be documented suggests that they are normal.[9]

Ironically, mainstream secular counseling panders to our insatiable appetite for ever more "positive" illusions, through building self-esteem—something diametrically opposed to authenticity and self-acceptance. In fact, such counseling is a *refusal* to accept the truth about ourselves.

We need to be converted from self-esteem to self-acceptance. God sends us trials so that we can see our true character and our great needs…so that He can wean us from self-trust (2 Corinthians 1:8-9; 4:7-18; 12:9-10; 1 Peter 1:6-7; Ecclesiastes 3:18). However, it is only through the promises of His unchanging love and forgiveness that we can tolerate such a revelation. Accordingly, Elyse M. Fitzpatrick, director of Women Helping Women Ministries, writes:

- The counter-intuitive truth that the depressed person needs to hear isn't "you're really a wonderful person," but rather, "you're more sinful and flawed than you ever dared believe"…Bathing our soul in the Gospel message will powerfully transform…It's true that I'm more sinful and flawed than I ever dared believe, and that truth frees me from the delusion that I'll ever be able to approve of myself; but I'm also more loved and welcomed than I ever dared hope, and that truth comforts and encourages me when my heart condemns me and my darling desires are all withheld.

It assures me that although I struggle with accepting myself, the Holy King has declared me righteous.[10]

It is only through God's acceptance that we can begin to accept the painful truth about ourselves and live authentically. Ironically, there is great freedom in this. If we can learn to rejoice in the pit, then we can enjoy our time on the mountaintop. If we can accept the unflattering portrait of ourselves, we can cease our obsessive and strenuous preoccupation with trying to prove ourselves. If we can accept ourselves, then the opinions of others lose their bite. Criticism will no longer constitute a threat because it can reveal no new dirt about who we are.

Self-acceptance is a pre-condition for authenticity. Modernity's answer is self-esteem, but that turns out to be the antithesis of self-acceptance. In fact, striving for self-esteem is actually a *refusal* to accept ourselves as we truly are.

EUDAIMONIA AND DEPRESSION

Mental health professionals recognize that living in accordance with our moral convictions is an important factor for mental health. Karen Wright has a definition that is helpful:

- Eudaimonia refers to a state of well-being and full functioning that derives from a sense of living in accordance with one's deeply held values.[11]

This is so obvious. Even atheists perceive this and are intent upon living moral lives. However, they ascribe their moral programming to evolution. For example, Richard Dawkins writes:

- Natural selection, in ancestral times when we lived in small stable bands like baboons, programmed into our brains altruistic urges, alongside sexual urges, hunger urges, xenophobic urges and so on.[12]

Consequently, from the point of view of evolution, altruism has nothing to do with truth or the idea of right and wrong, since it originates from meaningless and random processes. Why then should we follow these altruistic urges? Appealing to our genetic, biochemical impulses isn't adequate. For example, should we not follow our sexual impulses, even if they lead us into adultery or the abandonment of our families? Whichever we choose, this decision is solely the product of a cost/benefit analysis with our own welfare at the center of our calculations.

Besides, if "altruism" is no more than a biochemical reaction, it will eventually breed cynicism or self-righteousness. Why cynicism? For the atheist, the only possible rationale for living "virtuously" is self-fulfillment. Then, what happens when virtue no longer offers the same returns?

The practice of virtue, apart from truth, offers diminishing returns for our efforts. Consequently, we will quickly tire of virtue and the increasingly costly benefits. To increase the returns, virtue effortlessly morphs into something more permanent—self-righteousness—the conviction that "I am more worthy than others, because I am a good person."

Paul Kurtz—atheist, humanist, and author of the *Humanist Manifesto II*—affirms that pragmatism is the only possible justification for morality:

- How are these principles [of equality, freedom, etc.] to be justified? They are not derived from a divine or natural law nor do they have a special metaphysical [beyond the material world] status. They are rules offered to govern how we shall behave. They can be justified only by reference to their results.[13]

However, pragmatism isn't adequate. Sometimes it *isn't* pragmatic to be moral. Hiding Jews from the Nazis wouldn't pass the cost/benefit analysis. The price of a bullet in the head of an entire family is just too high. Therefore, non-theists cannot live in harmony with both their cost/benefit rationale and the law of God written upon their conscience (Romans 2:14-15). Either they hide Jews and violate their pragmatism…or they don't hide Jews and violate their conscience. Matters of the heart or conscience and matters of the pragmatic secular mind are divided and in conflict. No matter which choice the person in our hypothetical case might make, his mental well-being would suffer because he was unable to live, as Wright wrote, "in accordance with [his] deeply held values."

Ultimately, the one who denies God and therefore denies the moral absolutes of the conscience, will fail to derive the benefits of Eudaimonia, a sense of well-being. There is little satisfaction in living in accordance with the dictates of the conscience if we understand them to be no more than tyrannical, electro-chemical reactions. And, to add insult to injury, these same "virtuous" electro-chemical reactions demand that we make sacrifices that go against our immediate desires. These same virtuous impulses will then punish us with guilt feelings when we violate them. Is it any wonder that so many people are taking conscience-numbing drugs?

In contrast, for the Christian, the conscience and the Word—the heart and the mind together—represent the will of God, the source of all truth, joy, peace and love. We have every reason to regard it as a tremendous privilege to follow Him. Understandably, living according to His truth is a delight (Psalm 1:1-3; John 4:34).

MEANING, PURPOSE AND DEPRESSION

We are psychologically constituted to seek to understand our place in the world and to comprehend our purpose and meaning within it. The Jewish philosopher and theologian, Abraham Heschel, asserted this very thing:

- It's not enough for me to be able to say 'I am'; I want to know *who I am* and in relation to whom I live. It is not enough for me to ask questions; I want to know how to answer the one question that seems to encompass everything I face: What am I here for?[14]

However, not just any random understanding will do the trick. We need to understand that we are more than just an accident, a mere product of nature and nurture. The maverick psychologist, James Hillman, concurs:

- We dull our lives by the way we conceive them…By accepting the idea that I am the effect of…hereditary and social forces, I reduce myself to a result. The more my life is accounted for by what already occurred in my chromosomes, by what my parents did or didn't do, and by my early years now long past, the more my biography is the story of a victim. I am living a plot written by my genetic code, ancestral heredity, traumatic occasions, parental unconsciousness, societal accidents.[15]

If we fail to see ourselves as part of a *higher* narrative, there is a great danger of falling into depression. When we recognize that our lives have meaning, we can endure the trials and frustrations. Even the atheist and Christian-despiser, Frederick Nietzsche, wrote that:

- He who has a why to live for can bear almost any how.[16]

But from where does this "why," or rationale, come? Not from secular materialism, which denies all spiritual realities. In this regard, psychologist Arthur Deikman writes:

- Human beings need meaning. Without it they suffer…Western Psychotherapy is hard put to meet human beings' need for meaning, for it attempts to understand clinical phenomena in a framework based on scientific materialism in which meaning is arbitrary and purpose non-existent.[17]

This leaves us with one possibility—a self-created, existential meaning. The brilliant atheist mathematician Bertrand Russell was confident that he could create such a self-made reality and his own meaning to help him to live his life. In *Why I am Not a Christian*, he wrote of cherishing…

- …the lofty thoughts that ennoble his little day; disdaining the coward terrors of the slave of fate [of the rest of mankind], to worship at the shrines that his own hands have built; undismayed by the empire of chance."[18]

However, a self-constructed meaning is not sufficient. To suggest that one can merely dream up his own purpose is like telling someone that, instead of getting married he can merely dream up his own wife and kids for company. Instead, we need to *know* that we are somehow connected to Someone greater. Russell's self-created meaning failed to hold back the "coward terrors" of which he spoke. Subsequently, he admitted:

- I wrote with passion and force because I really thought I had a gospel. Now I am cynical about the [my] gospel because it won't stand the test of life.[19]

We were made to participate in a glorious drama (Jeremiah 29:11), and only acting on this exalted stage can ennoble and truly fortify us against depression (2 Corinthians 5:20-21).

GUILT, SHAME AND DEPRESSION

Depression is often the result of our unresolved and crippling feelings of guilt, shame and inadequacy. John Bradshaw warns about the depressing effect of these feelings—especially shame—which he defines as…

- The internalized feeling of being flawed and defective as a human being…shame, which should be a healthy signal of limits, becomes an overwhelming state of being, an identity if you will. Once toxically shamed, a person loses contact with his authentic self. What follows is a chronic mourning for the lost self.[20]

Bradshaw then explains how shame—"the master emotion"— begins to tragically numb the rest of the emotions through denial, repression, and dissociation. Where did this life-controlling shame come from? According to Bradshaw, it is a product of not being loved unconditionally. If this is the problem, then the answer is a matter of providing unconditional love. One way this is achieved is, once again according to Bradshaw, through loving affirmations:

- Repeated positive messages are emotional nutrients…Here are the loving words you can say to your inner infant:

  "Welcome to the world, I've been waiting for you. I'm glad you are here. I've prepared a special place for you to live. I like you just the way you are. I will not leave you, no matter what…"[21]

There are several problems with Bradshaw's approach:

1. Bradshaw assumes that toxic shame is always the result of a lack of love. Perhaps loving indulgence might make us less sensitive to feelings of guilt and shame, but this doesn't mean that an increased sensitivity is pathological. Instead, it might have a beneficial effect. Likewise, it might be better to live with our uncomfortable inhibitions, than to indulge ourselves at the expense of others.

Guilt and shame demand self-examination. If we have transgressed, the appropriate action is confession and repentance (1 John 1:8-9), not soothing self-talk. If sin is the problem, then Bradshaw's suggestion is merely a professional form of denial.

2. It's not believable. If positive affirmations are going to work, they must be believed, but they should only be believed if they are in harmony with reality! However, it's hard to take seriously Bradshaw's proposed affirmations: "I've prepared a special place for you to live. I like you just the way you are…"

3. Believing something silly can only provide minimal and temporary relief. On the other hand, if Bradshaw's affirmations can work to alleviate depression, how much more God's affirmations! If it helps me to hear the self-addressed words: "I will not leave you," how much more affirming to hear God

promise me His eternal presence (Romans 8:38-39; Hebrews 13:5)? If I am reassured by, "I like you just the way you are," I should find God's promise that He loves me with a surpassing love even more reassuring (Ephesians 3:17-20). Finally, I may be able to forgive myself, but God's forgiveness (Hebrews 8:12) will penetrate so much more intimately and persuasively, and will eventually secure my self-forgiveness.

Bradshaw's self-affirmations are to God's affirmations as masturbation is to true relationship—a substitute for the real thing. Even more pertinent, self-affirmations must be believed if they are to have any impact. However, Bradshaw promotes his suggested affirmations apart from any consideration of their truth-content. The mind and reality are thus compromised for the sake of fleeting emotional relief. If we stoop to unreality, we will pay a hefty price further down the road.

In contrast to this, the Bible doesn't admonish us to believe that Christ died for our sins simply so that we might derive a sense of relief, but primarily because *it is true*, as many reliable witnesses have attested. God's solution never requires us to compromise our intellectual integrity…or reality.

MORAL LIVING, BLESSING AND DEPRESSION

Lastly, moral living translates into blessing.

- "If you know these things, blessed are you if you do them." (John 13:17)

This blessing, of course, includes those who are depressed.

The relationship between obedience and blessing is no more clearly observed than in the context of marriage. Here we find that we best meet our own needs when we earnestly address the needs of our spouse (Ephesians 5:28; 1 Peter 3:7).

In this regard, it is interesting to see that the leading names in marriage counseling are counseling couples according to the very principles found in Scripture. Whereas psychotherapists had been jumping on the communication-techniques bandwagon as the means to address marital conflict, they are now returning to the concepts of love and respect. John M. Gottman, professor of psychology and co-founder of The Gottman Institute, writes:

- The typical conflict-resolution advice won't help. Instead, you need to understand the bottom-line difference that is causing the conflict between you—and learn how to live with it by honoring and respecting each other.[22]

Gottman claims that a year after the average couple graduates from a standard course of conflict-resolution training, only 18% retain any benefit from it. This represents a far smaller percentage than those marriages which spontaneously improve. Marriage guru, Harville Hendrix, concurs:

- Feel more loving toward each other simply by engaging in more loving behaviors…The husbands and wives are to grant each other a certain number of these caring behaviors a day, no matter how they feel about each other.[23]

The type of "other-centeredness" that Gottman and Hendrix advocate can certainly jump-start a languishing relationship. However, in the long run, more is needed. Loving your mate can be hard work. Besides, if we are just *giving* in order to *get*, the getting will eventually dry up, along with the giving. In fact, there may be long periods of time when we won't see any sort of payoff. This is why progress requires substantial effort, driven by deeply-held convictions, in order for one to commit to keep on going. Our focus must rest upon our spouse's needs. But how do we do this when our own needs go unmet?

Larry Crabb explains that this "humanistic foundation" sets us up for failure by placing the emphasis upon meeting our own needs.[24] Instead, if we are going to continue to act lovingly towards our mate, we need a true other-centeredness based upon the conviction that *it is right to do so*…even when we aren't getting what we want from the relationship. Furthermore, we will not be able to continue with this type of sacrifice unless we are assured that God is pleased, that He is taking care of us as we sacrifice our immediate comforts for the benefit of our mate.

If both sacrificial giving and going to the marriage counselor are only about getting results, then our efforts aren't truly giving. This kind of behavior is not likely to produce the kind of long-range results we want. Instead, our mate will perceive our behavior as manipulation—giving only in order to get what we want. The whole process will come to be seen for what it is—a thinly-concealed business transaction. "I am giving to you…so that I can be reimbursed."

What happens to the guy who brings his wife flowers whenever he wants sex? Eventually, she will see through his manipulation and resent his gift. The flowers, which were supposed to be signs of true romance and intimacy, will come to be seen as no more than payment for services rendered by her body.

What can lift couples out of such self-serving "altruism"? The conviction that their mission is far loftier than the immediate fulfillment of their needs. They are ambassadors of the God of all truth, wisdom, healing, and love (2 Corinthians 2:15; 5:20). They belong to Him (1 Corinthians 6:19-20). Consequently, they are no longer helpless depressives but servants of Glory (Galatians 2:20).

❖   ❖   ❖

There are many other psychological needs—forgiveness, humility, contentment, accomplishment, validation, joy, beauty and more—that we could survey in order to demonstrate how our Lord and His wisdom best address those needs. In contrast, there are numerous counterfeits. Curiously, they provide some relief in the short-run, but as with all drugs, there are hidden costs.

The wisdom of the Bible is uncanny. How is it that a collection of ancient books continues to nourish us in all the very specific ways we need? If the Bible didn't do this, we might well question whether it came from a superior Intelligence. However, in many ways, it bears the fingerprints of a God who loves us so much that He wants to share His mind with us.

WHAT MAKES NATIONS THRIVE AND OTHERS DIE?

CHAPTER SUMMARY

Only when we are assured of our riches in the next life will we make sacrifices in this one.

We rise and fall according to our beliefs. This principle pertains not only to individuals but also to nations. Previously, I have argued that if we live according to Biblical ideas and beliefs, we thrive. It is also obvious that if nations live according to Biblical ideas, they too will thrive.

Why do certain nations fail while others succeed, even abundantly? Indian economist Vishal Mangalwadi concluded that trustworthiness was a major factor. The following are some of the questions he asked himself as he conducted his research:

- Why are the Dutch or the English able to trust each other in a way that the Indians or the Egyptians cannot? What makes some cultures more honest, less corrupt, more trustworthy, and therefore more prosperous? And why is the postmodern West discarding the moral secret of its success?[1]

Mangalwadi became convinced that the way we believe is the way we behave. Indeed, our beliefs and behaviors have a direct impact on economic growth. He observed:

- People in the Netherlands had money to give because generation after generation was taught to work hard and give tithes and offerings to God. The Dutch made money to give to the poor in India because the Bible taught, "He who has been stealing must steal no longer, but must work, doing something useful with his own hands, that he may have something to share with those in need." (Ephesians 4:28)[2]

In contrast to the Christian worldview, Mangalwadi observed that Hindu philosophy is directly related to the impoverishment of India:

- India's religious philosophy taught that since the human soul was divine, it could not sin. In fact, our most rigorous religious philosophy teaches that everything is God. God is the only reality that exists, and therefore there is no ultimate distinction between good and evil, right and wrong.[3]

If we believe that we are gods, or part of the one god-consciousness, we do not believe in a standard higher than ourselves to which we must conform. Consequently, it is not wise to transact a business deal with someone who believes that he is above moral constraints. Instead, it is wiser to do business with someone who has a high commitment to moral truth and acts accordingly.

Mangalwadi discovered that economic and technological advances are inseparable from morality. Furthermore, he came to believe that morality is inseparable from religion, specifically the Christian religion. He lamented the fact that Hinduism had failed to provide an adequate moral foundation for India. This deficiency played itself out in a number of ways. Here is one example that he cites:

- Our [Hindu] monks did not develop technical aids to improve their eyesight. They took pride in closing even perfectly good eyes in meditation.[4]

Why did the monks with poor sight not get eyeglasses? The Hindu religion lacked those ideas that promoted the welfare of the people. For one thing, if this material world is illusory, then work and technological advancement are counter-productive:

- It is virtually impossible to find a Brahmin guru in traditional India who resembles the apostle Paul—a rabbi who made tents for a living. Brahmins said that manual work was the duty of lower castes, a result of bad karma from their previous births. Mahatma Gandhi was the first Indian leader who used a spinning wheel to try to import the Pauline work ethic into India: "No work, no food."[5]

The disdain for hard work kept India backward for centuries. However, it was technology and the Christian theology that inspired it that had enriched the West. Mangalwadi gives several examples:

- The peasants' humble wheeled plow generated the economic strength that helped save Europe from colonization by Islam. During the Middle Ages, Islamic forces were able to invade Europe almost at will. Muslims conquered southern Spain and Portugal and invaded France in the eighth century. In the ninth century, they conquered Sicily and invaded Italy, sacking Ostia and Rome in 846. By 1237, they had begun to conquer Russia. Constantinople was captured in 1453, and the battles of 1526 in Hungary and 1529 in Vienna suggested that it was merely a matter of time before the mullahs, caliphs, and sheikhs would rule cities like Rome, Vienna, and Florence. Equipped with a coulter, a horizontal share, and a moldboard, Europe's new plow increased productivity by tilling rich, heavy, and badly drained river-bottom soil...The net result was the gradual elimination of starvation, the improved health of the people, and a strengthening of the economic foundations of the West relative to Islam.[6]

The *Book of Proverbs* claims that "Righteousness exalts a nation, but sin is a disgrace to any people" (Proverbs 14:34). A heightened concern about sin and its evil power exalted the West. Conversely, could it be that sin and our denial of it is at the root of the current decline? Mangalwadi provides an illuminating example from his own country. In 1631, the seasonal monsoon had failed to come. As a direct consequence, there was a great famine. A British traveler relates the devastation he saw:

- From Surat to this place all the highway was stowed with dead people, our noses never free from the stink of them…women were seen to roast their children…a man or a woman no sooner dead but they were cut in pieces to be eaten.[7]

Mangalwadi reasoned, "My people did not starve because they were stupid, lazy, or unproductive." Instead, immorality killed them! They were taxed 80% of their produce. This left them with little, and nothing to store for an emergency. The only way for the people to have any money was to "join their exploiters."

Virtue exalts a people. Mangalwadi relates a revealing experience. Trying to purchase tickets from a machine on an Amsterdam tram, he was becoming increasingly frustrated by his lack of success. He asked a couple of American tourists for assistance. Here is what they said:

- "Why do you want to get tickets?" they responded. "We've been riding around for a week. No one has ever come to check our tickets."[8]

Mangalwadi was startled more by their hardness of conscience than by their theft-of-services:

- Their shamelessness shocked me more than their immorality. They represented the new generation, liberated from "arbitrary" and "oppressive" religious ideas of right and wrong. University education had freed them from commandments such as, "You shall not steal."[9]

Someone has to pay the price for sin. Eventually, the Dutch will have to hire additional personnel to collect the fares. Who will pay for this added expense? Everyone! I too have met many such travelers. They are intelligent, likeable, knowledgeable, highly-educated, and even sensitive to victimization in its various forms. But they are unable, unwilling—or both—to "connect the dots" to their own behaviors. Not a twinge of shame!

This kind of conduct serves as an omen of the coming tsunami that will inevitably submerge the economy, along with everything we value. It is already at our door, but no one sees it. When I talk about this coming destruction, my secular friends look at me as if I am from another planet. Instead, their hope is in this world, and it is just too difficult for them to question their unfounded expectations. Mangalwadi also marvels at what is happening in the West:

- This good news [of the Christian faith] became the intellectual foundation of the modern West, the force that produced moral integrity, economic prosperity, and political freedom. If moral integrity is foundational to prosperity, why don't secular experts talk about it? The reason is that the universities no longer know whether moral laws are true universal principles or mere social conventions made up to restrict our freedoms. And why don't they know? Economists have lost the secret of the West's success because philosophers have lost the very idea of truth. Why? The truth was lost because of an intellectual arrogance that rejected divine revelation.[10]

Moral truth has become a ball and chain. The West has long been in the process of removing the roots that had once nourished it. In many academic and intellectual circles, there is a palpable *disdain* for any objective moral dos-and-don'ts. The West wants to be free from such judgments. The West wants to be free from anything that indicates its culpability, anything that might elicit guilt or shame. Meanwhile, we continue to live off the accumulated wealth of generations that came before us, and most of us are unaware that it will soon disappear.

The quest for absolute freedom has made slaves of those who seek it, and this fruitless search has deprived them of their dignity as human beings. They are so intent to escape from guilt, shame, and the resulting negative self-image that they have adopted philosophies that will ultimately degrade them. They have exchanged the concept of human responsibility for the belief that we are simply products of our society and upbringing. They have convinced themselves that this worldview will set them free from their painful feelings.

Some even go a step further and entirely deny free will, opting instead for the belief that everything that we do has been pre-determined by biochemical events. Therefore, they claim that we should not feel guilty about anything we do, since we could not have done otherwise. Some are so enamored with this idea that they have become evangelists for their new faith. One gentleman with whom I have had considerable contact leads a group entitled, "The Illusion of Free Will." He insists that once we understand that free will is an illusion, we will be liberated.

If one believes that there is no free will, how easy it would be to cheat your business partner! After all, *you couldn't have acted otherwise*. With this mind-set, how easy it would be to give into any temptation. In the absence of any substantial rational resistance, we become slaves to our impulses.

- The evil deeds of a wicked man ensnare him; the cords of his sin hold him fast. He will die for lack of discipline, led astray by his own great folly. (Proverbs 5:22-23)

❖ ❖ ❖

Once we do wrong and refuse to admit it, we condemn ourselves to a never-ending pattern of rationalizations. Whether we deny our guilt through denying our free will, or through the many methods of "mindful" dissociation, such practices and deceits of the mind have never helped those nations that have practiced them.

Instead, the introduction of Jesus into a culture, even where conversions have been lacking, has edified that culture or nation. Robert Woodberry, a professor of sociology at the University of Texas, devoted 14 years to investigate why certain countries develop thriving democracies, while neighboring countries are failed states.

Woodberry discovered that a long-denigrated ingredient was actually central to the creation of successful states. The essential ingredient? The missionary. He writes:

- Areas where Protestant missionaries had a significant presence in the past are on average more economically developed today, with comparatively better health, lower infant mortality, lower corruption, greater literacy, higher educational attainment (especially for women), and more robust membership in non-governmental associations.[11]

In *America's Blessings: How Religion Benefits Everyone, Including Atheists*, Sociologist of Religion Rodney Stark provides further evidence that Christian love has profoundly impacted those among whom it has been planted. Jerry Newcombe, whose notes on Stark's work I am drawing from, writes:

- ✓ He [Stark] notes that religion benefits everyone, even the non-religious, who feel the residual effect.

- ✓ Those who attend church more often tend to donate much more often. For example, he writes, "...religious people dominate the ranks of blood donors, to whom even some angry humanists owe their lives."

- ✓ Religious Americans are far more likely to contribute even to secular charities, to volunteer their time to socially beneficial programs, and to be active in civic affairs.

- ✓ Religious Americans enjoy superior mental health—they are happier, less neurotic, and far less likely to commit suicide.

- ✓ Religious Americans also enjoy superior physical health, having an average life expectancy more than seven years longer than that of the irreligious. A very substantial difference in longevity remains even after the effects of "clean living" are removed.

✓ Religious people are more apt to marry and less likely to divorce, and they express higher degrees of satisfaction with their spouses. They also are more likely to have children.

✓ Religious husbands are substantially less likely to abuse their wives or children.

✓ Although often portrayed as ignorant philistines, religious Americans are more likely to consume and sustain "high culture."[12]

Such neighbors will inevitably exert a positive impact on their communities. In contrast, the Communist ideal has been to treat everyone in the same manner. However, each of their failed states suggests that brotherhood cannot be imposed from above, but must radiate out from concentric circles of intimacy. The old trope is true: "Love must begin at home, if it is to benefit anyone."

❖ ❖ ❖

I often ask people if we can learn *any* lessons from the past. The answer is usually, "No! The situation is different now and requires different solutions." Anticipating my next question—"What then has made the West successful?"—they skillfully avoid it. Why be encumbered by the lessons of the past if such reflection interferes with finding the "truth" within our own desires?

The following quote from a millennial might be a fair representation of what many young people are thinking today:

• Who would have dreamed of the internet 50 years ago? No one! In earlier times, who would have dreamed about TV or interplanetary travel? We therefore have learned to dream.

While there is a place for dreams, there is also a place for learning lessons from our past mistakes. But lessons are not as exciting as dreams. Idealistic dreams provide food for the ego, while a sober look at the past is humbling.

Chapter 25

It is noteworthy that Christian presuppositions have profoundly benefitted humanity. Meanwhile, modern, idealistic assumptions—which should have benefitted from the findings of science and history—have often plunged those they promised to help into chaos.

How is it that the Bible has captured such needful wisdom from goat-herders and fishermen? It is the contention of this book that they have been inspired by God.

CHARITY AND COMPASSION: A LEGACY OF CHRIST

CHAPTER SUMMARY

Historians—among them, Alvin Schmidt and Vishal Mangalwadi— have noted that charity and compassion have been embodied by Christianity above all other religions. How has this been possible? Only the Bible is able to provide an adequate foundation for the benefits that accompany true charity and compassion.

Charity did not have its origin in the world of antiquity:

- Plato (427-327 BC) said that a poor man (usually a slave) who was no longer able to work because of sickness should be left to die. He even praised Aesculapius, the famous Greek physician, for not prescribing medicine to those he knew were preoccupied with their illness (*Republic* 3.406d – 410a). The Roman philosopher Plautus (254 – 184 BC) argued, "You do a beggar bad service by giving him food and drink; you lose what you give and prolong his life for more misery" (*Trinummus* 2.338-39). Thucydides (ca. 460-44 BC), the honored historian of ancient Greece, cites an example of the plague that struck Athens during the Peloponnesian War in 430 BC. Many of the sick and dying of the Athenians were deserted.[1]

The Romans acted in much the same way until they were shamed into changing their ways by Christians who, during a plague, took in the Roman sick. This inspired their enemy, Emperor Julian the Apostate, to say:

- The impious Galileans [Christians] relieve both their own poor and ours...It is shameful that ours should be so destitute of assistance.[2]

The Christian faith was characterized by the other-centeredness of Christ-followers. According to B.B. Warfield:

- Hospitals and asylums and refuges for the sick, the miserable and the afflicted grow like heaven-bedewed blossoms in its path. Woman, whose equality with man Plato considered a sure mark of social disorganization, has been elevated; slavery has been driven from civilized ground; literacy has been given by Christian missionaries, under the influence of the Bible.[3]

Regarding the difference that Christ has made in the world, forgetfulness has dulled our confidence and worldview, but these are the facts:

- In the United States the spirit of charity in voluntary associations is greater among church members than among those who are not, according to a nationwide study conducted in 1987. Those belonging to Christian churches also give more financially to nonchurch charities, and they give a higher proportion of their income to such charities.[4]

Alvin Schmidt, author of *How Christianity Changed the World,* claims that this is the heritage of several hundred years of vigorous church preaching on charity:

- With these early American precedents, it is not surprising that astute foreign observers noted that the United States has, virtually from its inception, been a shining example of a charity-minded country…When Alexis de Tocqueville visited the United States in 1831, he astutely observed: "If an accident happens on the highway, everybody hastens to help the sufferer; if some great and sudden calamity befalls a family, the purses of a thousand strangers are at once willingly opened and small but numerous donations pour in to relieve their distress."[5]

In the 1890's, Amos Warner identified churches as "the most powerful agent in inducing people to give." Even as late as the 1940's, Gunnar Myrdal remarked:

- "No country has so many cheerful givers as America." He attributed this cheerful giving, or "Christian neighborliness," as he called it, to the "influence of the churches."[6]

Historically, charity and Jesus are inseparable. Frank Dekker Watson has concluded that:

- It is difficult to understand the great influence that charity exerted on the acts of man unless one realizes how religion, especially Christianity, has reinforced by its teachings the instinct of sympathy and altruism.[7]

Schmidt claims that this "cheerful giving" is still among us, to some degree:

- The amount that they [Christian families] gave to the poor and needy in 1991 amounted to $650 per American household. And in 1998 American church members contributed more than $24 billion to their churches, amounting to $408 per member.[8]

What has given the West its incredible vision and vitality? Carlton Hayes offers this:

- From the wellsprings of Christian compassion our Western civilization has drawn its inspiration, and its sense of duty, for feeding the poor, giving drink to the thirsty, looking after the homeless...[9]

Here is another quotation from Schmidt regarding the profound influence of Christianity on the advances of medicine in our world:

- The physician and medical historian Fielding Garrison once remarked, "The chief glory of medieval medicine was undoubtedly in the organization of hospitals and sick nursing, which had its organization in the teachings of Christ." Thus, whether it was establishing hospitals, creating mental institutions, professionalizing medical nursing, or founding the Red Cross, the teachings of Christ lie behind all of these humanitarian achievements. It is an astonishing mystery that the Greeks, who built large temples...never built any hospitals.[10]

The same was true for Rome, prompting historian Philip Schaff to assert that, "The old Roman world was a world without charity." Schmidt therefore concludes:

- Every time that charity and compassion are seen in operation, the credit goes to Jesus Christ. It is he who inspired his early followers to give and to help the unfortunate, regardless of their race, religion, class or nationality.[11]

Historian and physician Fielding Garrison recognized that...

- ...the credit of ministering to human suffering on an extended scale belongs to Christianity.[12]

Writing about the status and origins of medicine a bit closer to home, Schmidt writes that, early in the history of the United States, there were...

- ...no established medical institutions for nursing and ministering to the general populace...As the growth of hospitals spread across the nation, it was predominantly local churches and Christian denominations that built them...[However], the Christian identity and background of many American hospitals is now being erased.[13]

Today, secularists should be credited for having some compassion. However, we should remember that they are trying to replace the joyful and empowering giving of the Christian church with the enforced "giving" of impersonal entitlement programs. Schmidt reminds us that the secularists who enacted the social programs that were designed to help the poor "...had grown up under the two-thousand-year-old umbrella of Christianity's compassionate influence."[14]

Chapter 26

Likewise, Josiah Stamp claims:

- Christian ideals have permeated society until non-Christians, who claim to live a "decent life" without religion, have forgotten the origin of the very content and context of their "decency."[15]

Secularists are quick to claim credit for these advances that have affected every area of Western culture and society. Historian Rodney Stark contradicts this claim:

- ...the West is said to have surged ahead precisely as it overcame religious barriers...Nonsense. The success of the West, including the rise of science, rested entirely on religious foundations, and the people who brought it about were devout Christians.[16]

Indeed, there is a direct correlation between the moral and material rise of the West and the teachings of the Bible:

- Therefore, as God's chosen people, holy and dearly loved, clothe yourselves with compassion, kindness, humility, gentleness and patience. Bear with each other and forgive whatever grievances you may have against one another. Forgive as the Lord forgave you. (Colossians 3:12-13)

❖ ❖ ❖

What we believe matters. Vishal Mangalwadi's observations about his native India demonstrate the truth of the adage: "The way we think is the way we live." Our philosophies and worldviews are the foundations upon which we build our houses. Whether the "structures" we build are characterized by caring, or by chaos and destruction, is based upon what we believe. This very apparent truth can be demonstrated in any area of human endeavor. To illustrate the causal power of our philosophies, let's consider the area of medicine.

Mangalwadi has reported that India had pioneered a number of medical advances, including cataract surgery and plastic surgery. However, the fruitful study and practice of medicine enjoyed only a relatively brief span of time in India. Mangalwadi explains that medicine and even compassion lacked an adequate rationale in his homeland. Why was this so? The answer is, at least in part, because India's doctors were also regarded as "gurus" who could not be questioned:

- This attitude toward knowledge could not create and sustain an academic culture where peers and students could challenge, reject, and improve the medical techniques they had received. Thus, India had intellectual giants but our religious tradition failed to build academic communities. Individual genius, knowledge, and excellence in technology are insufficient to build a medical center.[17]

Mangalwadi also claims that Indian religions couldn't provide an adequate rationale for compassion—a necessary pre-condition for the practice of medicine:

- A person's suffering was believed to be a result of her or his karma in a previous life. In other words, suffering was cosmic justice. To interfere with cosmic justice is like breaking into a jail and setting a prisoner free. If you cut short someone's suffering, you would actually add to his suffering because he would need to come back to complete his due quota of suffering.[18]

Although Buddhism says a lot about compassion, according to Mangalwadi, its message is conflicted:

- The Buddha had to renounce his own wife and son to find enlightenment. He saw attachment as a cause of suffering. Detachment, therefore, became an important religious virtue…Those whose commitment was to their own spiritual enlightenment did not have the motivation to develop a scientific medical tradition.[19]

It is easy to see how the Buddhist understanding of "detachment" also led its adherents to detach from the sufferings of others.

Our ideas have wings, and the Biblical ideas flew the highest, according to Mangalwadi:

- The idea that the state should pay surgeons to serve the poor came to India with the Bible. Secularism hijacked the biblical idea, but it provides only the form, not the spirit. It is possible to bring a mango plant from India and grow it in Minnesota. One might even get a few crops. But under normal circumstances, the tree will not survive and certainly not reproduce.[20]

Secularism might be able to grow a mango tree in its own soil, but will it survive for long? Will compassion survive without its Christian roots? Indian medicine wasn't able to survive in its cognitive climate. Secularism claims to promote compassion, but will it fully survive once its other-centered Christian underpinnings are removed?

It doesn't seem that secularism has a firm enough basis for compassion. For one thing, it doesn't have a high view of humanity. Materialism and naturalism—components of today's secularism—regard humanity as just another animal, albeit more intelligent. However, some of us—babies, the mentally handicapped, and the delusional—aren't as intelligent as some animals. As a consequence, there are some among us who are becoming increasingly expendable in the West. This begs the question: Who else will join the ranks of those who are deemed to be expendable? Inevitably, materialism breeds elitism.

Besides, if we are regarded as no more than cosmically-purposeless animals, then there remains no reason to treat us as if we were anything more. Consequently, in some secular societies, especially in the twentieth century, dissidents and other "malignant elements" were exterminated with the same zeal as one might swat and kill annoying mosquitos.

Moral relativism, the child of materialism, eliminates the possible existence of any human or unalienable rights. Morals simply become human inventions which are granted and rescinded at will, according to the prevailing agenda of the secular State.

Secular multi-culturalism is born out of moral relativism. It maintains that we have no rock-solid basis upon which to judge other cultures or even to defend our own. For example, in blatant contradiction with their own purported values, some nations in the secular West have even gone so far as to allow the establishment of Sharia courts. These courts render judgments that are in stark opposition to the very rights the West has committed itself to uphold.

Such moral confusion cannot continue to provide an adequate foundation for the rights that we enjoy—the unalienable rights that have caused the West to prosper and thrive.

❖   ❖   ❖

Malcolm Muggeridge, the late British journalist and former secular humanist, observed:

- I've spent a number of years in India and Africa where I found much righteous endeavor undertaken by Christians of all denominations; but I've never, as it happens, come across a hospital or orphanage run by the Fabian [communist] society, or a humanist leper colony.[21]

Why not? Their undergirding philosophy/religion fails to support such structures, unless they are politically expedient. Why is it that Christianity embodies the very values that promote human welfare? Perhaps these values come from Above.

As we watch Christian values continue to erode, we should also expect to see the erosion of everything that is based upon these values—relationships, trust, cooperation, diligence, business, and even science. The crimes and financial scandals of today will come to look like nursery games compared to those we will see tomorrow.

THE CHRISTIAN MISSIONARY: THE BEARER OF GOD'S GIFTS

CHAPTER SUMMARY

Christian missions have gotten a bad and undeserved rap. Nevertheless, they have transformed many cultures for the better. How? Christian missionaries came bearing the truth, God's Gospel.

If you doubt that Christian missions have been maligned by secular media, just watch a PBS or BBC history special on the subject. The missionaries who followed in the wake of the Conquistadores have received special condemnation. If anyone were to watch a BBC TV series called *The Missionaries,* he or she would hear claims like the following:

- "Under the guise of evangelism came harsh exploitation and eventually the enslavement of the Indians."

In *6 Modern Myths about Christianity and Western Civilization,* research fellow Philip J. Sampson attacks the myth that the missionaries were oppressors. He counters that many of the missionaries had taken a strong stance against the colonial powers. He cites a sermon by Dominican Antonio de Montesinos (1511), who preached against the sins of the white colonists:

- "Tell me, by what right and with what justice do you keep these poor Indians in such cruel and horrible servitude? By what authority have you made such detestable wars against these people?…you kill them with your desire to extract and acquire gold every day…Are these not men?…Are you not obliged to love them as you love yourselves?"[1]

Contrary to the philosophy of Aristotle, who regarded the slave as a "live tool," the Bible grants dignity to all humanity as "…created in the likeness of God" (Genesis 1:26). Sampson points out the consequence of this:

- Many 19th century missionaries were appalled at the slave trade and did their best to try to change it. William Burns opposed the 'coolie' trade in China and protested to British government representatives…Missionaries in East Africa were horrified at the local slave trade and were at a loss as to what to do about it.[2]

In her discussion about the missionaries to Africa, historian Ruth Tucker acknowledges that, while there were missionaries who also understood their role as one of westernizing the natives…

- …They, more than any other outside influence, fought against the evils colonialism and imperialism brought. They waged long and bitter battles…[against] the heinous traffic in human cargo. And after the demise of the slave trade they raised their voice against other crimes, including the bloody tactics King Leopold used to extract rubber from the Congo. The vast majority of missionaries were pro-African, and their stand for racial justice often made them despised by their European brothers. Indeed, it is no exaggeration to say that without the conscience of Christian missions, many of the crimes of colonialism would have gone entirely unchecked.[3]

Referring once again to Sampson, he explodes the myth that missionaries were in collusion with the imperialists and colonists. In fact, the missionaries were often expelled by the colonial powers to prevent them from "publicizing atrocities or intervening to help the native people."[4] He agrees with Tucker:

- Missionaries in Africa were opposed to slavery from an early period, and they used a variety of means to oppose it, including buying slaves and establishing plantations for them to work on.[5]

According to Sampson, rather than collusion, conflict characterized missionary-colonialist relations:

- The missionaries insisted on treating native people as human beings who are entitled to the protection of the law, and this rubbed salt into the wound. It should come as no surprise, therefore, that colonists and traders often opposed missions.[6]

- Traders and colonists resisted the evangelism of native people, seeing conversion as the first step to indigenous people gaining access to the resources of Western culture and hence to the power that colonists wished to keep for themselves...Native people who wished to break free of the settler's stranglehold and worship God were immediately persecuted by the white traders.[7]

Stephen Neill's *History of Christian Missions* gives an example of this:

- The missionaries [to New Guinea] from the start found themselves in bitter opposition to the white traders and exploiters, whose attitude was expressed by one of them to John G. Patton in the words "our watchword is 'Sweep these creatures away, and let the white men occupy the soil,'" and who, in pursuance of their aim, placed men sick of the measles on various islands in order to destroy the population through disease.[8]

In contrast to the concerns of the missionaries, the educated elites disdained the idea of the spiritual equality of all the various races of Christians and aligned themselves with the exploiters. This was not the viewpoint of the missionaries, as can be seen in the following quote:

- Missionaries, on the other hand, were ridiculed in scholarly journals for their shallow thinking in regard to race.[9]

Another important factor in this discussion is the fact that Darwinism had made racism intellectually respectable. Evolutionist Karl Giberson acknowledged the prevailing racism:

- How shocking it is today to acknowledge that virtually every educated person in the Western culture at the time...shared [evolutionist] Haeckel's [racist] ideas. Countless atrocities around the globe were rationalized by the belief that superior races were improving the planet by exterminating defective elements...there can be little doubt that such viewpoints muted voices that would otherwise have been raised in protest.[10]

As a consequence, evolutionists presented no rationale to oppose the abuses of colonialism. In contrast to this, Tucker cites A.F. Walls:

- But one thing is clear. If missions are associated with the rise of imperialism, they are equally associated with the factors which brought about its destruction.[11]

She also cites Ralph Winter:

- Protestant missionary efforts in this period led the way to establishing all around the world the democratic apparatus of government, the schools, the hospitals, the universities and the political foundations for the new nations.[12]

What greater testimony to the contributions of missionaries could there be than their dedication among those with whom they worked! Nevertheless, they have often been charged with the destruction of native culture. This is ironic because, among so many other benefits, missions have done more than any other group to codify and preserve indigenous languages:

- The anthropologist Mary Haas estimates that 'ninety per cent of the material available on American Indian languages, is missionary in origin.[13]

Admittedly, in some ways the missionaries did oppose indigenous cultures. For example, they campaigned against certain native practices, like female circumcision. No less a luminary than Charles Darwin confessed:

- Human sacrifice...infanticide...bloody wars, where the conquerors spared neither women nor children—all these have been abolished...by the introduction of Christianity.[14]

Why then all the bad press against the missionary? Once again, let's see what Darwin had to say:

- Disappointed in not finding the field of licentiousness quite so open as formerly, they [the Western traders] will not give credit to a morality which they do not wish to practice or to a religion which they undervalue, if not despise.[15]

Consequently, the historian Stephen Neill concludes:

- [The] Weight of the evidence tells heavily against the accusation that missionaries have been responsible for the destruction of native cultures.[16]

Christian missionaries bravely opposed the prevailing worldview. Representative of the Darwinian thinking of his day, Richard F. Burton complained that the Christian willingness to treat Africans as "...men and brethren [was] a dangerous error at odds with the evolutionary facts."[17]

Instead of such heresy, we see example after example of missionaries swimming against the tide of the erroneous thinking of their day:

- [Faith in the Gospel]...Encouraged Dr. John Philip of the London Missionary Society to support native rights in South Africa in the early nineteenth century...[Faith in the Gospel encouraged] Lancelot Threlkeld to demand equal protection under the law for the Awabakal people of Australia and also inspired John Eliot to persuade the Massachusetts courts to find in favor of native people against settler claims. Even so unsympathetic an author as David Stoll concedes that the contemporary missions in Latin America 'tended to treat native people with more respect than did national governments and fellow citizens.'[18]

This should be no surprise. It has been faithfulness to their beliefs that has motivated Christians from the start. Regarding this, Philip Yancey provides some insights that he gleaned from the historian Rodney Stark:

- In the midst of a hostile environment, the Christians simply acted on their beliefs. Going against the majority culture, they treated slaves as human beings, often liberating them...When an epidemic hit their towns, they stayed behind to nurse the sick. They refused to participate in such common practices as abortion and infanticide. They responded to persecution as martyrs, not as terrorists. And when Roman social networks disintegrated, the church stepped in. Even one of their pagan critics had to acknowledge that early Christians loved their neighbors 'as if they were our own family.'[19]

❖ ❖ ❖

Nevertheless, the many secular charges against missions have taken their toll. Hwa Yung, the bishop of the Methodist Church of Malaysia, is concerned about the waning of Western missions. He cites Western guilt and charges of "imperialism" as major culprits, and he wants to counteract these misguided allegations. For one thing, intellectuals from newly established countries...

- ...Long for their countries to become modern democracies with advanced economies. They do not buy into the secularization theory that suggests that the unique, finely balanced combination of democracy, political stability with checks and balances in government, civil society, human rights undergirded by a strong and just legal system, and an advanced economy with minimal corruption will emerge willy-nilly with modernization. They have looked at the 20th century experiment called Marxism, perhaps the most secular of ideologies, and have found it utterly wanting for either the prosperity or the freedoms they seek.[20]

This conclusion should be a matter of common sense, but it certainly isn't common. Oddly, the secularists of the Western university credit secularism with Western successes. Meanwhile, they have substituted moral relativism for a commitment to moral truth and absolutes. Now these same secularists are stunned at the various moral, economic, social and political woes that are afflicting the West. This is because they are unwilling to give credit where credit is due:

- These intellectuals have reached the same conclusions as those of the late American legal scholar Harold Berman and the sociologist Rodney Stark: The moral values, legal principles, and psychological basis of the best modern Western civilizations came from their Christian history. Thus, many, like Chinese cultural Christians, see the gospel alone as able to provide adequate moral foundations for rejuvenating their nations.[21]

Oddly, we in the West have lost sight of this truth. In fact, it has even become politically incorrect to make such observations. Those who do may find that their livelihoods are imperiled.

Bishop Yung cites a 2008 article in *The Times* (UK) by Matthew Parris, a journalist and former British MP, reflecting on his visit to Malawi:

- Now a confirmed atheist, I've become convinced of the enormous contribution that Christian evangelism makes in Africa: sharply distinct from the work of secular NGOS, government projects and international aid efforts. These alone will not do. Education and training alone will not do. In Africa Christianity changes people's hearts. It brings spiritual transformation. The rebirth is real. The change is good...Those who want Africa to walk tall amid 21st[st] century global competition must not kid themselves that providing the material means or even the knowhow that accompanies what we call development will make the change. A whole belief system must first be supplanted by another. Removing Christian evangelism from the African equation may leave the continent at the mercy of a malign fusion of Nike, the witch doctor, the mobile phone, and the machete.[22]

That is all well and good, but some might be wondering: Haven't Christian missions undermined indigenous culture? Isn't there indeed at least some solid ground for Western guilt? Yung cites Yale professor Lamin Sanneh, who claims that Christian missions actually helped to preserve cultures and languages. This was accomplished through the translation of the Bible into vernacular languages:

- As he put it, "Christian missions are better seen as a translation movement, with consequences for vernacular revitalization, religious change and social transformation, than as a vehicle for Western cultural domination." I don't know of any serious scholar refuting Sanneh's thesis.[23]

If we are concerned about the advancement of the Third World, then missions should be encouraged. Besides, all of this should give renewed emphasis to Jesus' parting instructions to His followers:

- Then Jesus came to them and said, "All authority in heaven and on earth has been given to me. Therefore go and make disciples of all nations, baptizing them in the name of the Father and of the Son and of the Holy Spirit, and teaching them to obey everything I have commanded you. And surely I am with you always, to the very end of the age." (Matthew 28:18-20)

Christian missions have arguably been a tremendous source of positive change. It is therefore a pity that they have been so maligned. Instead, we find that where the missionaries have trod, so too has come abundance.

In view of all this, we should ask, "Why hasn't communism or Hinduism produced such benefits within the nations where they have spread?" Perhaps they came with ideas—and with 'gods'—that failed to promote the people...while Christianity came with ideas that proved to be salutary for their hosts.

Still another question remains to be answered: Why is it that these truths have proven to be so beneficial? Perhaps they came from Above, from the one benevolent God.

Chapter 28

THE RISE OF THE CHRISTIAN WEST— THE FALL OF THE SECULAR WEST

CHAPTER SUMMARY

Today, it is common to hear how Christianity is the source of almost every evil. The Christian faith is even considered to be the major obstacle to scientific advancement. As these errant ideas take root in the now-secular West, people are more tempted than ever to abandon the Church. Therefore, a counter-narrative should be considered.

It has almost become a career-killer for a professor to laud the fruits of the Christian faith. Instead, it seems as if every day we hear the voices of those who hold that Christianity is the source of almost every evil. In ever-widening circles, Christianity is viewed as a major obstacle to advances in science. As these false narratives take root in the West and people are tempted to abandon the Church, let us consider a counter-narrative.

Historian Rodney Stark writes that:

- The success of the West, including the rise of science, rested entirely on religious foundations, and the people who brought it about were devout Christians.[1]

Secularism is often erroneously associated with science and scientific advancement. However, regarding the Scientific Revolution, Stark writes:

- Some wonderful things were achieved in this era, but they were not produced by an eruption of secular thinking. Rather, these achievements were the culmination of many centuries of systematic progress by medieval Scholastics, sustained by that uniquely Christian twelfth century invention, the university. Not only were science and religion compatible, they were inseparable—the rise of science was achieved by deeply religious Christian scholars.[2]

Many people cite Greece and Rome as proof that democracy has little to do with Christianity, that even our democratic roots aren't Christian, but Classical. Stark shines some much-needed light on the mindset of some of the greatest Classical thinkers:

- The rules that Plato laid out concerning the proper treatment of slaves were unusually brutal, for he believed not that becoming a slave was simply a matter of bad luck but that nature creates a "slavish people" lacking the mental capacity for virtue or culture, and fit only to serve.[3]

Consequently, only the worthy were suitable for Greek "democracy":

- [Aristotle] Drew upon Plato's biological claims—slavery is justified because slaves are more akin to dumb brutes than to free men: "From the hour of their birth, some are marked out for subjection, others for rule."[4]

In contrast, democracy finds its sufficient and enduring foundation in the Biblical concepts of human respect and our essential equality. The third century Christian theologian L. Caecilius Firmianus Lactantius wrote:

- The second constituent of Justice is equality. I mean this...in the sense of treating others as one's equals...For God who gives being and life to men wished us all to be equal...But someone will say, "Don't you have poor and rich"...Not at all! This is precisely the reason that we address one another as "Brother," since we believe that we are one another's equals [despite the superficial differences]. Since human worth is measured in spiritual and not in physical terms, we ignore our various physical situations: slaves are not slaves to us, but we treat them and address them as brothers in the spirit, fellow slaves in devotion to God. Wealth, too, is no ground for distinction, except insofar as it provides the opportunity for preeminence in good works. To be rich is not a matter of having, but of using riches for the tasks of justice...By conducting oneself not merely as the equal of one's inferiors, but as their subordinate, one will attain a far higher rank of dignity in God's sight.[5]

It is no surprise that, given the Classical understanding of humanity, democracy could not endure for long. Sadly, now as our Christian roots are decaying, so too are our democratic principles and productivity. Stark concludes:

- Without a theology committed to reason, progress and moral equality, today the entire world would be about where non-European societies were in, say, 1800: A world with many astrologers and alchemists but no scientists. A world of despots, lacking universities, banks, factories, eyeglasses, chimneys, and pianos. A world where most infants do not live to the age of five...The modern world arose only in Christian societies. Not in Islam. Not in Asia. Not in a "secular" society—there having been none. And all the modernization that has since occurred outside Christendom was imported from the West, often brought by colonizers and missionaries.[6]

❖ ❖ ❖

It is amazing that the apostles of secularism continue to confidently wave the banner of "progress" as the West implodes.

The West is experiencing an auto-immune reaction. It has virulently turned against its own roots. In its arrogance, it believes that it can create a superior world by demolishing the old. For example, it has replaced Christian mercy missions with secular NGOs—Non-Government Organizations. However, in an article entitled, "As an Atheist, I Truly Believe Africa Needs God," British journalist and professed atheist Matthew Parris—whom I also quoted in the last chapter—makes the following observations:

- [To...] leave the continent [Africa] at the mercy of a malign fusion of Nike, the witch doctor, the mobile phone and the machete instead of Christian missionaries is an act of violence.

Africa needs God...Missionaries, not aid money... [They] are the solution to Africa's biggest problem—the crushing passivity of the people's mindset.

Now a confirmed atheist, I've become convinced of the enormous contribution that Christian evangelism makes in Africa: sharply distinct from the work of secular NGOs, government projects and international aid efforts. These alone will not do. In Africa Christianity changes people's hearts. It brings a spiritual transformation. The rebirth is real. The change is good.

Christians, black and white, working in Africa, do heal the sick, do teach people to read and write; and only the severest kind of secularist could see a mission hospital or school and say the world would be better without it. I would allow that if faith was needed to motivate missionaries to help, then, fine: but what counted was the help, not the faith.[7]

According to Parris, there are hardcore secularists who will not give credit where the credit is due. However, Parris, who had spent his childhood in Malawi, knows otherwise:

- It inspired me, renewing my flagging faith in development charities. But travelling in Malawi refreshed another belief, too: one I've been trying to banish all my life, but an observation I've been unable to avoid since my African childhood. It confounds my ideological beliefs, stubbornly refuses to fit my worldview, and has embarrassed my growing belief that there is no God."[8]

The West too is "trying to banish" this belief. It does not want to be reminded of the fact that the supporting institutions of the West have been built with Christian hands. We see another example of this in the fact that the vast majority of colleges in the USA were founded by Christians, for Christian purposes:

- Of our 119 first colleges and universities, 104 were founded to teach biblical values…Even public universities commonly had Christian roots.[9]

These same schools have not only disowned any association with their Christian roots, they have turned bitterly against the mother who birthed them.

❖ ❖ ❖

Meanwhile, some non-Western scholars look on, incredulously. Former editor of the *Sunday Telegraph*, Dominic Lawson, in a review in the *Sunday Times* of Niall Ferguson's book, *Civilisation: The West and the Rest*, shares the following quotes about the source of the success of the West:

- One of the things we were asked to look into was what accounted for the success, in fact, the pre-eminence of the West all over the world.

  We studied everything we could from the historical, political, economic, and cultural perspective. At first, we thought it was because you had more powerful guns than we had.

  Then we thought it was because you had the best political system. Next we focused on your economic system.

  But in the past twenty years, we have realized that the heart of your culture is your religion: Christianity. That is why the West is so powerful.

  The Christian moral foundation of social and cultural life was what made possible the emergence of capitalism and then the successful transition to democratic politics. We don't have any doubt about this.[10]

We should take special note of who it was that said these things. It isn't from a spiritual leader or a religious think-tank. It is from a member of the Chinese Academy of Social Sciences. This Academy is an instrument of the Chinese Communist government, which spends a considerable amount of time and money persecuting Christians and is officially atheistic. If this is the conclusion it has come to, perhaps the West needs to reconsider its own biases.

Just to drive home the point, Lawson also refers to the fact that Wenzhou, the Chinese city which is rated as the most entrepreneurial in the country, is also home to 1,400 churches. Lawson quotes a prominent Wenzhou business leader, Hanping Zhang, who argues that "an absence of trust had been one of the main factors holding China back."[11] But Zhang feels that he can trust his fellow Christians—he knows that they will be honest in their dealings with him.

Trust must be the cornerstone for business, development, and all of our endeavors. However, it is a child that Secularism believes it can rear without her mother.

❖ ❖ ❖

A recent graduate from Yale Divinity School expressed her outrage at this "chauvinistic" thinking: "You have no right to claim that Christianity has borne better fruit than other religions or cultures." She then cited the supposed catalogue of the Church's misdeeds—the Crusades, colonialism, the witch trials, and even the World Wars.

However, even today, the fading Christian West is still regarded as a leader in many areas, like justice and social justice. If this is so, we need to ask, "Why?" If it is because of its Christian roots, we need to examine why these roots have nourished us so well. Could it be that these roots are being fed from the wellsprings of a God who loves us... a God Who is showing us off to the world as a model of what His love can accomplish?

Chapter 28

If this is so, then we should expect to see the drying-up of this wellspring as the Christian faith is rejected and marginalized. This is exactly what we find in cycles of decay—revival—and decay, as the next chapter illustrates.

Chapter 29

ALEXIS DE TOCQUEVILLE, MORALITY, DEMOCRACY, AND EVIDENCE FOR THE GOD OF THE BIBLE

CHAPTER SUMMARY

Alexis de Tocqueville wrote DEMOCRACY IN AMERICA in 1835.[1]
In his book, de Tocqueville credited Christianity for much of the
American marvel that he had observed while living in this country.

Today's secularism is an aggressive bulldozer. It will not tolerate any competition. It pushes aside any opposition to its reign. Arrogantly, it believes that it can retain the benefits of Western civilization while discarding its foundation—Christianity.

Alexis de Tocqueville, French statesman, historian, social philosopher and author of *Democracy in America*...would have disagreed. All of the quotations in this chapter have been taken from de Tocqueville's book. It has been described as "the most comprehensive and penetrating analysis of the relationship between character and society in America that has ever been written" (Robert Bellah).[2]

De Tocqueville wanted to understand why the American Revolution and American democracy had proven to be such a success. According to de Tocqueville, freedom and morality both found their American incarnation in Christianity:

- Religion in America...must be regarded as the foremost of the political institutions of that country; for if it does not impart a taste for freedom, it facilitates the use of it.

De Tocqueville had been well-acquainted with the demands for freedom and equality that had arisen from his own French revolution, which ironically had entailed the hatred and murder of the clergy. This revolution had confidently sought to push aside anything that stood in its way. However, with the advantage of decades of hindsight, another revolution was something that the French wanted to avoid at all costs. With the tumultuous lessons of his homeland still vivid in his mind, de Tocqueville wrote:

- The safeguard of morality is religion, and morality is the best security of law and the surest pledge of freedom.

He therefore appreciated the moral constraints that he found so ubiquitously associated with democracy in the United States:

- I do not question that the great austerity [self-control] of manners that is observable in the United States arises, in the first instance, from religious faith...its influence over the mind of woman is supreme, and women are the protectors of morals. There is certainly no country in the world where the tie of marriage is more respected than in America or where conjugal happiness is more highly or worthily appreciated...

Over and over again, he found that the fruitful expression of democracy was inseparable from its underlying Christian roots:

- In the United States the influence of religion is not confined to the manners, but it extends to the intelligence of the people...Christianity, therefore, reigns without obstacle, by universal consent; the consequence is, as I have before observed, that every principle of the moral world is fixed and determinate.

De Tocqueville's glowing observations of Christian faith and conduct did not amount to a claim that Christianity had rooted out all evils. It certainly hadn't—but neither had any other religion or government. Slavery remained a troubling example. But in view of the many moral failures in every nation and the worldwide acceptance of slavery, this one failure should not be used to discredit the entirety of the Christian influence on America.

Chapter 29

According to de Tocqueville, the greatness of the United States was the outgrowth of what the churches were preaching:

- I sought for the key to the greatness and genius of America in her harbors...in her fertile fields and boundless forests; in her rich mines and vast world commerce; in her public school system and institutions of learning. I sought for it in her democratic Congress and in her matchless Constitution. Not until I went into the churches of America and heard her pulpits flame with righteousness did I understand the secret of her genius and power. America is great because America is good, and if America ever ceases to be good, America will cease to be great.

In contrast, today's secularism believes that it can retain the fruits of Christian society without any practical application of its roots. It seeks to replace the Christian foundation with its own materialistic and relativistic presuppositions, vainly expecting that these will support the house of their dreams. Secularism wants to retain the ideas of equality and equal protection under the law—the Bill of Rights—but it fails to see that their materialistic foundation cannot support the structure they hope to build.

Historically, materialism has not been able to provide the bedrock foundation for these prized values. Just look at the various supposedly worker-centered "utopias" that have been implemented by communist, atheistic nations. Why have these societies been so characterized by oppression and violence? From a strictly materialistic frame of reference, *there can be no possible basis for equality or "unalienable rights."* After all, some people are tall and some are short; some are likable and some are not; some promote justice, while some undermine it; some contribute to society, while some prove to be detrimental, even undermining the common good. Consequently, as seen through the materialistic lens, some people have a positive value and some a negative one. Therefore, is there any basis for equality from this perspective? Not at all.

Christians also have a materialistic lens; however, *we are not limited to this lens*. We also have a transcendent one. We see equality and the surpassing value of humanity—even of the murderer—because this is the reality that God sees. We protect because God protects…even the most unworthy. We maintain that all have unalienable rights because all have been created in the likeness of God. Therefore, we cannot deprive anyone of their rights because these rights don't come from us—they come from God.

However, according to the lens of secularism, it is secularism that grants the rights. Consequently, it is secularism that can also retract those rights, as we see happening now. There is nothing in a materialistic worldview that requires that our rights be *unalienable*. After all, everything is in flux, and so our rights as well should be subject to the whims of the State.

Even worse, there is nothing in secular materialism that would argue in favor of equal treatment for all. If some people have a positive social value in that they contribute to the welfare of society, and some have a negative social value—according to a materialistic worldview, there is no justification for not treating the negatively-valued people in a negative way. Consequently, materialism cannot truly and honestly value equality and unalienable human rights.

The same argument can also be applied to the concept of "freedom." Where there is no solid, foundational basis for equality, there is also no basis for the equality of freedom for everyone. After all, some people vote "Republican" and are against gay marriage. Why should their ideas be tolerated? As secularism secures its grip, any ideas that impede its agenda are no longer tolerated. The popular vote can be overturned by a single judge. The charge of "unconstitutional" can be brought against any objectionable idea, or even against the results of an election.

The secularism of today has lost its taste for freedom as the quest for self-fulfillment has proliferated. De Tocqueville warned that democracy is vulnerable in this regard:

- Men who are possessed by the passion of physical gratification generally find out that the turmoil of freedom disturbs their welfare before they discover how freedom itself serves to promote it.

What is not honored—our freedoms and liberties—will eventually wither and disappear. De Tocqueville realized that the pursuit of a perverted conception of "equality" could indeed produce some bad fruit:

- But there exists in the human heart a depraved taste for equality, which impels the weak to attempt to lower the powerful to their own level, and reduces men to prefer equality in slavery to inequality with freedom.

The argument in favor of "equality" can be applied in many illegitimate ways. It can be used to produce "equality" between parents and their children, depriving parents of their rightful authority in favor of the Secular State. It can be used as a bulldozer to push aside any sexual distinctions. Consequently, it is argued that we should be allowed to marry or to have sex with anyone—and any number of them—we please. Once again, from the perspective of a materialistic worldview, it is only our appetites that should set the limit. Meanwhile, there is no longer a willingness to regard the many studies that have unequivocally demonstrated that children—and society—do far better in a myriad of ways, with their biological parents.

Our personal comforts, pleasures and proclivities tend to reign over concerns about distant abstract principles, such as freedom and justice. Therefore, de Tocqueville warned:

- A democracy cannot exist as a permanent form of government. It can only exist until the voters discover that they can vote themselves largesse from the public treasury. From that moment on, the majority always votes for the candidates promising the most benefits from the public treasury with the result that a democracy always collapses over loose fiscal policy, always followed by a dictatorship. The average age of the world's greatest civilizations has been 200 years.

❖ ❖ ❖

Democracy is a fragile flower, which requires regular cultivation. History is the test tube for our ideas, and the future will cast its dispassionate verdict on those ideas. It will also give us what we deserve. Already, anti-Christian secularism is bearing its fruit in terms of abortions, STDs, suicides, criminality, and broken families throughout the Western world.

We will reap what we sow and sadly, we will probably find that de Tocqueville's words have proved to be prophetic:

- The safeguard of morality is religion, and morality is the best security of law and the surest pledge of freedom.

Does this analysis prove the truth of the Christian faith? We should ask ourselves: How is it possible that this ancient book—the Bible—has produced such good fruit? Why have the "truths" of communism, National Socialism, and Islam produced such devastation, while the teachings of the Bible have produced human flourishing?

Sadly, most will only hear the final verdict after it is too late.

REVIVAL: CHRISTIANITY'S FALL AND RISE IN ENGLAND

CHAPTER SUMMARY

When the Christian voice revives, society thrives; when it is silenced, society decays. The history of Western nations is a testimony to what happens when its Christian voice is silenced. We can see this clearly from the record of what happened in early 18th century England.

Indian Scholar Vishal Mangalwadi writes:

- In 1738, two centuries after the Reformation, Bishop Berkeley declared that religion and morality in Britain had collapsed "to a degree that was never before known in any Christian country." The important reasons for the degeneration of Protestant England were the restoration of the monarchy and the supremacy of the Anglican Church at the end of the seventeenth century. Once the Anglican Church came back to power, it began to oppress the Puritans and expelled more than four hundred conscientious Anglican clergymen. They had become priests to serve God, and therefore they refused the oath of allegiance to William of Orange.[1]

With this compromise, the Anglican priesthood became utterly corrupt:

- A succession of archbishops and bishops lived luxuriously, neglecting their duties, unashamedly soliciting bishoprics and deaneries for themselves and their families. Parish clergy followed suit...Corruption spread like cancer.[2]

The Church is the conscience of society. When it is silenced, corruption and moral decay are free to spread to all the segments of a society. Mangalwadi continues:

- The moral darkness of the age expressed itself in a perverted conception of sport, which, like alcohol, brought attendant evils in its train, such as further coarsening of the personality, cruelty, and gambling.

  As for lawlessness, thieves, robbers, and highwaymen, Horace Walpole observed in 1751, "One is forced to travel, even at noon, as if one were going to battle." Savagery showed itself in the plundering of shipwrecked vessels, lured by false signals onto rocks, and in the indifference shown to the drowning sailors. This was a regular activity along the entire coastline of the British Isles.[3]

Similarly, it appears that whenever the Christian influence is compromised by serving a second master—as Jesus taught in Matthew 6:24—social ills have multiplied.

However, there were also revivals. Into this English malaise stepped the preachers John Wesley, John Whitefield, and others like them. It must be said that their ministry to the poor and downtrodden was not appreciated at first. No one likes their sins to be exposed or their positions to be threatened. Mangalwadi's chronicle continues:

- For three decades, magistrates, squires, and clergy turned a blind eye to the continual drunken and brutal attacks by mobs and gangs on Wesley and his supporters. Wesley endured physical assault with missiles of various kinds. Frequently bulls would be driven into the midst of the congregations or musical instruments blared to drown out the preacher's voice. Time after time, the Wesleys and Whitefield narrowly escaped death, while several of their fellow itinerant preachers were attacked and their homes set on fire. Hundreds of anti-revival publications appeared, as did regular, inaccurate, and scurrilous newspaper reports and articles. And the most virulent attacks, not surprisingly, came from the priests, who referred to Wesley as "that Methodist," "that enthusiast," "that mystery of iniquity" [anti-Christ], "a diabolical seducer, and imposter and fanatic."[4]

The foulest criticism is always clothed with a thin veneer of decency and concern for the "rights and needs" of others. How else can a corrupt establishment appeal to the masses, apart from disguising their cause as moral and just? Despite the fierce opposition, Wesley and Whitefield persevered:

- The biblical revival affected the lives of politicians. Edmund Burke and William Pitt were better men because of their Bible-believing friends. They helped redefine the civilized world...Perceval, Lord Liverpool, Abraham Lincoln, Gladstone, and the Prince Consort, among others, acknowledged the influence of the Great Awakening. The biblical revival, beginning among the outcast masses, was the midwife of the spirit and character values that have created and sustained free institutions throughout the English-speaking world. England after Wesley saw many of his century's evils eradicated, because hundreds of thousands became Christians. Their hearts were changed, as were their minds and attitudes, and so society—the public realm—was affected.

  The following improvements came in a direct line of descent from the Wesleyan revival. First was the abolition of slavery and the emancipation of the industrial workers in England. Then came factory schools, ragged schools, the humanizing of the prison system, the reform of the penal code, the forming of the Salvation Army, the Religious Tract Society, the Pastoral Aid Society, the London City Mission, Muller's Homes, Fegan's Homes, the National Children's Home and Orphanages, the forming of evening classes and polytechnics, Agnes Weston's Soldier's and Sailor's Rest, YMCAs, Barnardo's Homes, the NSPCC, the Boy Scouts, Girl Guides, the Royal Society of Prevention of Cruelty to Animals and the list goes on. Ninety-nine out of a hundred people behind these movements were Christians.[5]

This redemptive story has been repeated many times throughout the history of the Church. Here's how one person described the impact of the revival in Wales in 1904:

- Judges were presented with white gloves: they had no cases to try. No rapes, no robberies, no murders, no burglaries, no embezzlements, nothing. The District Consuls held emergency meetings to discuss what to do with the police, now that they were unemployed. Drunkenness was cut in half. The illegitimate birth rate dropped 44 percent in two counties within a year of the beginning of the revival.[6]

❖   ❖   ❖

If Christianity has been such a potent engine for progress and reform, why then is it so widely despised today? Perhaps this observation by Charles Darwin concerning the impact of the work of missionaries will be helpful:

- I believe that, disappointed in not finding the field of licentiousness quite so open as formerly, [the traders in foreign mission fields] will not give credit to morality which they do not wish to practice or to a religion which they undervalue, if not despise.[7]

If it interferes with our pleasures and power, then discredit it!

When we place our orchids under lights, they thrive. When we thrust them into darkness, they eventually wilt. As many times as we repeat this experiment, the results remain the same. When the Christian faith flourishes, so does society; when it is suppressed, society decays. Evidently, there is something light-giving about this incredible faith and the God who stands by it.

PROOF OF THE GOSPEL FROM WHAT WE ALREADY KNOW ABOUT OURSELVES

CHAPTER SUMMARY

As strange as this might sound, every single one of us already knows the Gospel. It has been implanted within our DNA.

- For what can be known about God is plain to them, because God has shown it to them. For his invisible attributes, namely, his eternal power and divine nature, have been clearly perceived, ever since the creation of the world, in the things that have been made. So they are without excuse. (Romans 1:19-20, ESV)

So, we have the truth but reject it:

- The coming of the lawless one is by the activity of Satan with all power and false signs and wonders, and with all wicked deception for those who are perishing, because they refused to love the truth and so be saved. (2 Thessalonians 2:9-10)

Even though we reject and refuse the truth, we are drawn to the underlying message of the Gospel—the theme of the rejected, persecuted One coming back against all odds to save his people. This, of course, is a portrait of Jesus.

However, there are other ways and means by which the Gospel is revealed to us:

1. We know that there is something wrong with us; we even know that we deserve punishment.

2. We know that our lives are controlled by the insatiable need to cover over our problems and to convince ourselves that we are worthy and deserving. We do this through a variety

of inadequate strategies, seeking human validation rather than divine mercy.

3. We hunger for an ultimate solution.

Let me try to explain each of these three points…

1. We know that there is something wrong with us; we even know that we deserve punishment.

The Bible declares that we already know the truth about ourselves—that we are sinners who automatically try to suppress or rationalize our sins:

- For when Gentiles, who do not have the law, by nature do what the law requires, they are a law to themselves, even though they do not have the [written] law. They show that the work of the law is written on their hearts, while their conscience also bears witness, and their conflicting thoughts accuse or even excuse them on that day when, according to my gospel, God judges the secrets of men by Christ Jesus. (Romans 2:14-16)

Furthermore, when we sin, the sin-alarm goes off. We feel guilty and ashamed. We even experience the terrifying prospect of judgment. We try to cover over our transgressions, just as Adam and Eve did when they sinned in the garden. Yet, the manner in which we "cover up" today is just as flimsy and inadequate as the fig leaves of our first parents.

Those who believe in evolution are aware of these truths. They too acknowledge that every one of us is wired to have an uncomfortable reaction when we do something "wrong." Instead of acknowledging that God created us this way, those who believe in evolution describe the uncomfortable reaction to our wrong-doing as a mindless biochemical process.

Even if we believe that we have been wired by evolution, the sin-reaction—the uncomfortable feeling that we have done something wrong—remains powerful, even life-controlling. We live our entire lives trying to successfully manage this damning reaction. We are in an endless wrestling match, trying to deny our guilt by suppressing our feelings, "medicating" ourselves, or by trying to compensate for it in a myriad of different ways. We point to our attainments and acclaim, the wealth we have accumulated, our power or our popularity. All of the above are metrics by which we hope to prove to the world that we are worthy human beings, even when our deepest feelings are screaming out that we are not.

In *The Significant Life*, attorney George M. Weaver illuminates our ever-present need to establish our positive significance. For example:

- Salvador Dali once said, "The thought of not being recognized [is] unbearable"…Lady Gaga sings, "I live for the applause, applause, applause…the way that you cheer and scream for me." She adds in another song, "Yes we live for the Fame, Doin' it for the Fame, Cuz we wanna live the life of the rich and famous."[1]

Writer Gore Vidal was also unabashedly transparent about this:

- Whenever a friend succeeds, a little something in me dies.[2]

We are so controlled by the need to prove ourselves that we destroy our peace of mind and even our relationships. How can we explain this ruinous quest which robs us of our peace? Perhaps our preoccupation with our affirmations and achievements is the way we fight back against the feeling that we are undeserving and unworthy. However, this way of living one's life can only cover over the problem *and never eradicate it completely.* The core issue is never eliminated. Once again, we are like Adam and Eve, trying to cover over our sense of guilt and shame—all to no avail. Worthless "coverings" for sin didn't work then and they don't work now.

❖   ❖   ❖

Weaver also points to an even more bizarre attempt at regaining a sense of worthiness…through an act of absolute infamy:

- In 2005 Joseph Stone torched a Pittsfield, Massachusetts apartment building…After setting the blaze, Stone rescued several tenants from the fire and was hailed as a hero. Under police questioning, Stone admitted, however, that he set the fire and rescued the tenants because, as summarized at trial by an assistant district attorney, he "wanted to be noticed, he wanted to be heard, he wanted to be known."[3]

Evidently, this drive to cover our guilt and shame is so powerful that it can overrule the moral dictates of conscience. One mass-murderer explained in his suicide note:

- "I'm going to be f____ing famous."[4]

This drive for esteem can over-shadow all other affections. On December 8, 1980, Mark David Chapman, a zealous fan of the Beatle, John Lennon, first obtained his idol's autograph before gunning him down. He explained:

- "I was an acute nobody. I had to usurp someone else's importance, someone else's success. I was 'Mr. Nobody' until I killed the biggest Somebody on earth." At his 2006 parole hearing, he stated: "The result would be that I would be famous, the result would be that my life would change and I would receive a tremendous amount of attention, which I did receive…I was looking for reasons to vent all that anger and confusion and low self-esteem."[5]

What's wrong with having low self-esteem? Why can't we live with an accurate assessment of ourselves rather than an inflated, distorted one? Low self-esteem tends to reaffirm what we already know about ourselves—that there is something wrong with us. This provokes feelings of unworthiness and dread. Consequently, no matter how high our self-esteem, we still live in fear of failure and rejection, which tends to invalidate us.

Many have devoted themselves to the practice of virtue in order to feel that they are good and deserving. However, from what I have observed, those people are well-aware that their chosen way is fundamentally self-serving. In fact, they tend to become even more aware of their moral deficiencies as they strive to be virtuous. Consequently, Buddhists—those totally committed to right-living—have little hope of ever reaching nirvana, the presumed bliss of nothingness. Even as they vainly strive to improve their karma, they live in fear that their next reincarnation will be downward.

The Bible confirms the fact that the moral law, imprinted upon our hearts, condemns rather than commends us:

- Now we know that whatever the law says it speaks to those who are under the law, so that every mouth may be stopped, and the whole world may be held accountable to God. For by works of the law no human being will be justified in his sight, since through the law comes knowledge of sin. (Romans 3:19-20)

Whatever our self-management strategy might be, we remain aware of the fact that something is terribly wrong with us. Even if we convince ourselves that the dis-comfort we sense when we sin is no more than a meaningless biochemical reaction, we spend our lives trying to prove our worthiness. What we might deny with our mouths, we affirm with our lives. Sadly, the whole time we are riding this insane merry-go-round, the self-condemnation never goes away.

However, our problems go far deeper than this. For, no matter how hard we try to convince ourselves otherwise, we cannot shake the impression that we actually deserve to be punished:

- Though they know God's righteous decree that those who practice such things deserve to die, they not only do them but give approval to those who practice them. (Romans 1:32)

Knowing that we deserve punishment, it is not surprising that many are contemptuous of the idea of a God. Atheist Aldous Huxley once confided:

- I had motives for not wanting the world to have meaning; consequently, I assumed it had none, and was able without any difficulty to find reasons for this assumption...For myself, as no doubt for most of my contemporaries, the philosophy of meaninglessness was essentially an instrument of liberation...*We objected to the morality because it interfered with our sexual freedom.*[6]

We know the truth of the Gospel but deny it because we feel judged by it. That is why Huxley embraced and found refuge in the "philosophy of meaninglessness," which he used as a shelter from truth and judgment. However, denial of the truth is not freedom from the truth. Those who deny the truth are constantly on guard against it. They remain defensive even when accused of a small wrong, such as cutting in line in front of someone else. As C.S. Lewis observed, such a person would not say, "I am an evolutionist and don't believe in such objective moral laws." Instead, this same person would try to defend himself when charged with his wrong-doing. The fact that he endeavors to defend himself is a tacit acknowledgment of an objective, implanted moral law. Although he would not admit it, he knows that such truths provide the basis for a meaningful life.

This understanding also helps to explain masochism—harming or denying oneself. When we indulge ourselves in something that we enjoy, we often feel an increase in stress. Why do we feel this way? We sense that we don't deserve any pleasure, and therefore we feel more blameworthy, even deserving of punishment.

Continuing to explore this idea, when people harm themselves— like those who are "cutters"—they often experience a temporary reduction of stress. Why would this be so? If our internal script is informing us that we deserve punishment—and we then oblige and punish ourselves—we are left with a fleeting sense that we have atoned for our sins.

> **2. We know that our lives are controlled by the insatiable need to cover over our problems and to convince ourselves that we are worthy and deserving. We do this through a variety of inadequate strategies, seeking human validation rather than divine mercy.**

There are many indications of this. We continue to lust after the approval of others no matter how much acclaim and success we have already achieved.

The richest man in the world was asked, "How much more money would you need to be satisfied?" J.D. Rockefeller answered, "Always a little bit more." This illustrates the fact that our solutions are only temporary at best. We are so addicted to our quest for validation that we need increasingly greater "fixes" in order to maintain our sense of well-being.

In *The Book of Esther*, Haman had become the second most powerful man in the Persian Empire. Whenever he passed by, everyone bowed down before him except one—the Jew Mordecai. This so enraged the insatiable Haman that he set about to have every Jew in the empire exterminated.

No matter how rich, respected, powerful or accomplished we might become, we will always crave more. Once again, we are like drug addicts forever trying to experience our initial high. However, our attempts to validate ourselves are no better than over-the-counter aspirin, which is unable to address the underlying cause of our stress.

Many are aware of the fact that the struggle to prove our worthiness and significance imprisons us. Many have rightly concluded that the attainment of any validation must be based on something beyond our self-centered achievements.

Our addictions are life-controlling. We remain so vulnerable that we cannot handle criticism. Instead of taking responsibility for our wrong-doing, we blame others. We become jealous when anyone else receives acclaim and recognition instead of us.

3. We hunger for an ultimate solution.

Many people realize that their strategies for finding peace have failed. Therefore, some have turned to spiritual solutions beyond themselves. There are even some people who acknowledge that there must be a payment for our sins. Here are some signs of this awareness:

- ✓ We try to do good, and there is some satisfaction in what we do. But we soon discover that any euphoria is temporary, and the effort expended is arduous. Even though this is the right thing to do, ultimately, it is not what we need. It is just another way for us to purchase a very short-lived sense of well-being.

- ✓ When we harm or at least deny ourselves, we experience temporary relief from feelings of guilt and shame. This is a clear indication that we are aware that we deserve punishment.

- ✓ When we sincerely confess our sins, we also find relief. This is true even when the wronged parties refuse to accept our apologies. We find that the honesty and humility of apologizing for our wrongs is healing. However, we are also aware that this relief only lasts until our next moral failure. This as well points us to the fact that there must be something more.

- ✓ The major religions of the world recognize these truths and the necessity of obtaining the complete mercy of a deity. But how is this to be done? Often, people create idols of wood and stone that they can easily placate with their daily offerings. However, we know in our hearts that we can never be good enough for God, despite our many sacrifices to attain good karma. Yet, the futility of our position forces us to "overcome" it with trophies of our superiority and moral worthiness. However, these mere tokens of worth only end up making us arrogant, judgmental, and self-righteous.

✓ We long to be loved unconditionally, despite our failings. However, we have also found that human relationships cannot provide this for us in any deeply satisfying way. This leads many to begin to search for One who can.

The Bible is also aware of these truths:

• For since the law has but a shadow of the good things to come instead of the true form of these realities, it can never, by the same sacrifices that are continually offered every year, make perfect those who draw near. Otherwise, would they not have ceased to be offered, since the worshipers, having once been cleansed, would no longer have any consciousness of sins? But in these sacrifices there is a reminder of sins every year. For it is impossible for the blood of bulls and goats to take away sins. (Hebrews 10:1-4)

Aware of this, the Buddhists long for the coming of the Second Buddha. The Muslims long for their deliverer, known by some as the Mahdi. The Jews long for their Savior, the Messiah.

❖ ❖ ❖

Any of our own efforts to achieve peace are destined to fail. Our God is so perfect in holiness and righteousness that there is nothing that we can give Him that will satisfy Him and atone—make adequate payment—for our sins. When we try to attain peace with God by our own means, there will always be a pervasive awareness that we have not been truly cleansed of our sins. We might go so far as to give alms of everything we have. We might even sacrifice our lives and yet still remain in bondage (1 Corinthians 13:3). When we come to the end of ourselves—our ideas and plans and machinations—we come face-to-face with the acute awareness that we need the mercy of God.

It is only through Jesus that our sins can be utterly eradicated. Then we can serve our God in joy rather than from a sense of compulsion. Only He, God incarnate, is the adequate payment for our sins:

- Therefore, brothers, since we have confidence to enter the holy places by the blood of Jesus, by the new and living way that he opened for us through the curtain, that is, through his flesh, and since we have a great priest over the house of God, let us draw near with a true heart in full assurance of faith, with our hearts sprinkled clean from an evil conscience and our bodies washed with pure water. Let us hold fast the confession of our hope without wavering, for he who promised is faithful. (Hebrews 10:19-23)

Perhaps this "proof" is the most important of all the proofs. However, the more we are disconnected from ourselves and our feelings, the more we remain unconvinced. Nevertheless, I think this proof might demonstrate to some—those who are being drawn—that the Gospel is the missing piece in their puzzle. Perhaps for others, it might serve as a seed that will later germinate.

DO GREAT CLAIMS REQUIRE GREAT EVIDENCES?

CHAPTER SUMMARY

In fact, great and small claims alike require relevant, trustworthy, supporting evidence. In the case of Christianity, great evidences are available, far more so than for naturalism.

Atheists generally say that the existence of God is a great claim, and that great claims require great evidence.

Actually, I tend to agree. However, I would insist that the evidence for the Creator should be examined and compared with the competing "great claim"—that natural forces are the "creators," that natural forces brought about the physical world as we know it. Both of these are extraordinary claims, and both require extraordinary evidence. One point of agreement between these two camps is that both agree—whether it was natural forces or a Creator responsible for the material world—that entity must be eternal and uncaused. This is an important factor in this discussion because, by this premise we can avoid the conundrum of infinite regress— an illogical and endless series of causes that would stretch back into infinity. For more on that, take another look at Chapter 11.

Of the two schools of thought represented here, I think that the God hypothesis has far more support. From the little that we understand, here are some observations:

1. Natural forces cannot explain the creation of matter, energy, time, or space. Instead, creation by natural forces would require the eternal pre-existence of all these elements— matter, energy, time, and space—before any natural forces could have acted upon them. However, if we consider just one of the above elements—time—we are confronted with an insurmountable problem: time cannot be eternal. An infinite number of years would have to be fulfilled before we could arrive at the present—a logical impossibility.

2. Natural forces cannot explain their own elegance, easily seen in the simplicity of their formulaic statements. Instead, the indisputable elegance we find in the structure and operation of the natural world suggests Intelligent Design.

3. Natural forces cannot even explain their own immutability in a world of molecules-in-motion. In such a world, we would expect these forces to change. However, if natural forces were in fact in a state of continual flux, there could be no science. Any kind of learning or research would be impossible.

4. The eternal Cause must be adequate to account for the rest of the universe. The omnipotent God hypothesis can explain everything. However, those who believe in natural forces as that cause are hard-pressed to account for many things— life, consciousness, freewill, objective moral law, or even the existence of a single atom.

5. *There is absolutely no evidence* that anything has ever been caused by a non-intelligent and non-designed natural force. Perhaps instead, these natural forces were created by God, emanate from His Being, and are not at all natural.

6. Knowing all of the above, it is more reasonable to assume the eternal existence of one creative Force, rather than an explanation that includes many natural forces.

❖ ❖ ❖

Admittedly, those who believe in theism and Intelligent Design have made other great claims, as well. For example, there is the belief in miracles—one-time phenomena that go beyond the grasp and purview of science. Question: Should miracles require extraordinary supportive evidence?

At this point, we need to make a necessary distinction between a single miracle and miracles in general. Miracles in general already possess extraordinary supportive evidence in the form of numerous supporting testimonies or reports.

But where are the scientific evidences against miraculous occurrences? They do not and cannot exist! Why not? Because science can only address repeating events, events that can be retested. But miracles are anomalous, one of a kind. Therefore, they cannot be repeated. It is therefore not appropriate to ask for scientific proof for things outside of the reach of science. Therefore, science cannot disprove miracles.

What do we make of the claims for individual miracles, like the Bible's insistence on the Virgin Birth? From a materialistic and naturalistic perspective, the Virgin Birth would require extraordinary evidences, but not from the perspective of Intelligent Design. If there is a God, then all of His creations are miraculous and thus transcend the grasp of science to explain their origin.

In light of this, we are taken back to the original question: "Does the Creator exist?" If He does, then He Himself is the extraordinary supportive evidence. How? This single Divine hypothesis can account for everything, while naturalism can reasonably account for nothing.

This doesn't mean that we should not be diligent about examining miraculous claims. In fact, the Bible tells us to examine all things, including ourselves. Even though we have a God who can perform miracles as easily as He can speak, the Bible also requires that any event or charge be established by at least two witnesses.

However, as I have argued earlier, even miracles, by themselves, can do little to change minds. After Jesus raised Lazarus from the grave after four days, instead of considering the implications of what they had just seen, many consorted to have both Lazarus and Jesus put to death (John 11). This account, and many others, demonstrates that people have the ability to deny or distort any form of evidence. Therefore, don't be surprised that the anti-supernatural bias is often deeply embedded and can stubbornly resist argumentation and piles of counter-evidence.

WHY DOESN'T GOD PROVIDE STRONGER EVIDENCES?

CHAPTER SUMMARY
He does. We just need to open our eyes to see them.

I am often confronted with this argument:

- If god really wanted me to believe in him, he would have provided more evidence.

As I have tried to argue in this book, He has already provided it…with flashing neon lights! Paul argued that the evidence is so compelling that we are "without excuse" if we reject it:

- For what can be known about God is plain to them, because God has shown it to them. For his invisible attributes, namely, his eternal power and divine nature, have been clearly perceived, ever since the creation of the world, in the things that have been made. So they are without excuse. (Romans 1:19-20, ESV)

Of course, the skeptic disputes that humanity could be so utterly blind to the evidence for God. However, most people are like the bulimic teen who is convinced that she is fat, even though she is continually told that she is not. She can observe herself in a mirror, but even the visual evidence does not change her self-perception.

We are surrounded by the evidence of God but cannot or will not see it. As a seven-year-old, I was exposed to the Lord's Prayer in my public school. When I would get into bed at night, I would clasp my hands together and pray that whole prayer in Jesus' name. Astonishingly, many incredible things happened for this seven-year-old. However, once I turned eight, I learned that I was Jewish, and that Jews didn't do that sort of thing. Therefore, I quit praying entirely. I had placed my ethnicity above what I *knew* about God, reaping disastrous consequences.

How are we to understand such a thing? Why did my ethnic identity take precedence over what I knew through experience? It certainly was not the case that God had disappointed me.

The experimental evidence that humanity is in denial about unwanted knowledge is rampant. In a 2007 *New York Times* article, "Denial Makes the World Go Round," Benedict Carey, by virtue of the overwhelming evidence, concludes:

- "The closer you look, the more clearly you see that denial is part of the uneasy bargain we strike to be social creatures," said Michael McCullough, a psychologist at the University of Miami and the author of the coming book *Beyond Revenge: The Evolution of the Forgiveness Instinct*. "…we cut corners to get individual advantage, and we rely on the room that denial gives us to get by, to wiggle out of speeding tickets, and to forgive others for doing the same."

  Everyone is in denial about something; just try denying it and watch friends make a list. For Freud, denial was a defense against external realities that threaten the ego, and many psychologists today would argue that it can be a protective defense in the face of unbearable news, like a cancer diagnosis.[1]

Perhaps we are also in denial about God—the One who makes moral demands and judges us when we fail to obey them.

Within the world of clinical psychology, observations of denial are extensive and perhaps most apparent in the field of addiction:

- The concept of denial calibrates widely shared ideas about language with the clinical regimen that characterizes mainstream American addiction treatment. Since the 1930s, denial has stood at the ideological center of the field and has enjoyed a wide range of professional adherents across otherwise distinctive theoretical orientations. As in so many contemporary addiction treatment programs, the professionals I studied believed that addicts are—by definition—unable to clearly see themselves. By extension, they also believed that addicts are unable to speak about themselves and their problems authoritatively.[2]

Psychologist Shelley E. Taylor writes that denial does not just apply to the addict, but to humanity as a whole:

- As we have seen, people are positively biased in their assessments of themselves and of their ability to control what goes on around them, as well as in their views of the future. The widespread existence of these biases and the ease with which they can be documented suggests that they are normal.[3]

Perhaps denying the evidence for God might also be a product of our biases. God not only interferes with our autonomy, awareness of Him also brings disruptive guilt feelings.

Psychologist Roy Baumeister has extensively researched the relationship between high self-esteem and performance. He concludes:

- There are now ample data on our population showing that, if anything, Americans tend to overrate and overvalue ourselves. In plain terms, the average American thinks he's above average. Even the categories of people about whom our society is most concerned do not show any broad deficiency in self-esteem.[4]

In other words, we have a great capacity to believe those things that make us feel good and to deny those realities that threaten our self-esteem and autonomy. This also pertains to the evidence for God, as even skeptics have admitted:

- We take the side of science in spite of the patent absurdity of some of its constructs...in spite of the tolerance of the scientific community for unsubstantiated commitment to materialism...we are forced by our *a priori* adherence to material causes to create an apparatus of investigation and set of concepts that produce material explanations, no matter how counterintuitive, no matter how mystifying to the uninitiated. Moreover, that materialism is absolute, for we cannot allow a Divine Foot in the door.[5]

- Even if all the data point to an intelligent designer, such a hypothesis is excluded from science because it is not naturalistic.[6]

❖ ❖ ❖

The resistance to the evidence for God is well-documented, but what can explain it? Jesus taught that God's existence is very threatening:

- "And this is the judgment: the light has come into the world, and people loved the darkness rather than the light because their works were evil. For everyone who does wicked things hates the light and does not come to the light, lest his works should be exposed." (John 3:19-20)

We cannot allow the truth about who we really are to be exposed. Truth is painful, as the *Book of Proverbs* points out:

- Wisdom cries aloud in the street, in the markets she raises her voice; at the head of the noisy streets she cries out; at the entrance of the city gates she speaks: "How long, O simple ones, will you love being simple? How long will scoffers delight in their scoffing and fools hate knowledge? If you turn at my reproof, behold, I will pour out my spirit to you; I will make my words known to you. Because I have called and you refused to listen, have stretched out my hand and no one has heeded, because you have ignored all my counsel and would have none of my reproof." (Proverbs 1:20-25)

Why do we refuse to listen to wisdom's rebuke? Because it humbles us, revealing our true identity and conduct. But this is the only way that true wisdom can begin its work in us—by correcting us. That is how the lens through which we see everything else is wiped clean. Only then can we really see.

Admittedly, even we Christians can become insensitive to the evidence around us. As a result, we too cry out to God: "Why don't You strengthen my faith? Reveal Yourself to me in a miraculous manner!"

Interestingly, we are in good company. Even while surrounded by Jesus' miracles, His disciples were unable to incorporate what they had observed into their worldview. Therefore, even they had asked Him to increase their faith (Luke 17:5). When John the Baptist was languishing in prison, racked with doubts, he asked his disciples to go to Jesus to ascertain if He really was the Messiah (Matthew 11).

The problem was not that they had been granted insufficient reasons to believe. John had seen the Spirit descend upon Jesus. He had identified Him as "the Lamb of God who takes away the sin of the world." The Apostles had seen hundreds, perhaps thousands of Jesus' miracles, and yet they still doubted. What then was their problem?

I think that John the Baptist and the Apostles had become humanly calloused in their hearts. Therefore, the problem was not a lack of evidence, *but a lack of fully integrating the evidence into their daily lives.* The same holds true for us. Because of our callousness, the Bible warns that we are not to forget what God has done for us. According to the Psalmist, Israel's problem was not that there was little evidence of God's mercy. Instead, the Israelites had willfully forgotten what they already knew:

- They did not keep God's covenant, *but refused to walk according to his law.* They forgot his works and the wonders that he had shown them. In the sight of their fathers he performed wonders in the land of Egypt, in the fields of Zoan. He divided the sea and let them pass through it, and made the waters stand like a heap. (Psalm 78:10-13)

I find that I too must mentally rehearse what God has done for me. I must be vigilant to remember His multiple evidences. It has been out of these many rehearsals that this book was born.

CHRISTIANITY AND CULTURE: CONSEQUENCES OF THE DIMINISHING CHRISTIAN INFLUENCE

CHAPTER SUMMARY

The West still retains some semblance of Biblical thinking and habits. However, as these characteristics of our culture continue to diminish, so too will many of the principles that we all cherish.

A leading atheist speaker recently informed her audience that it is possible for society to appropriate Christian principles—like equality—without the Christian religion.

Can we? I don't think so. There are principles that secularism, atheism, materialism and naturalism—which I will refer to as SAMN—will not be able to sustain for long. In fact, these principles are now quickly disappearing from the Western worldview: Human Primacy, Equality, Human Rights, Free Will, Justice, Objective Moral Law, and Meaning/Purpose.

HUMAN PRIMACY

Our legal systems give priority to humanity. Therefore, swatting a mosquito or cutting down a tree is not yet a criminal offense.

- Whoever sheds the blood of man, by man shall his blood be shed, for God made man in his own image. (Genesis 9:6)

It is thus clear from the Scriptures that human life has been given an honored standing in the hierarchy of the natural world. We were made in God's own image. However, SAMN provides no adequate basis to regard human life as more valuable than the life of a mosquito. Outside of the authority of the Bible, there is no way to rationally establish human value above that of anything else in the created world.

Consequently, many are saying, "All life has equal value." Against this, various measures of value are put forth—degrees of intelligence, creativity, or love. These criteria do not work. It is impossible to apply them consistently. According to standards like these, people who have more intelligence are esteemed to be more highly-valued than those with less.

HUMAN EQUALITY

With the demise of Biblical faith, there is no reason to regard each human being as equal before the law. From a SAMN point of view, we are unequal according to any possible measure—age, sex, strength, intelligence, societal contributions, even likeability, and more. Therefore, abortion, euthanasia, and many other social evils have now become rampant.

Our former cultural norm regarding the sanctity of all human life has morphed into a "Quality of Life" worldview. Seen through this lens, society has determined that some are less valuable than others, and therefore, more expendable. As this slide continues, it is inevitable that, because of supposed quality of life concerns, some people will be regarded as having less protection under the law.

HUMAN RIGHTS

SAMN has no adequate rational basis to place human rights above the rights of a pig. Instead, SAMN regards human rights as something that are granted by the State, not God. However, if the State is the entity that grants these rights, the State could just as easily retract them, especially if it no longer sees them as expedient. Instead of such a morally bankrupt state of affairs, the

Preamble of the Declaration of Independence proclaims the following:

- We hold these truths to be self-evident, that *all men are created equal, that they are endowed by their Creator with certain unalienable Rights*, that among these are Life, Liberty and the pursuit of Happiness.

The founders of our country understood that if our rights depended upon government to grant them, they could never be regarded as "unalienable."

FREE WILL AND CULPABILITY

SAMN provides no basis for a belief in free will. If there is no free will, there can be no guilt, courage, or integrity. People would act and respond to life only because of biochemical reactions. These reactions would determine every choice we make and all the different ways that we behave. Here is what author Daniel C. Dennett has to say about that:

- ...free will, in their view, is obviously incompatible with naturalism, with determinism, and very likely incoherent against any background, so they cheerfully insist that of course they don't have free will, couldn't have free will, but so what?[1]

Therefore, according to this way of thinking, we are little more than highly-sophisticated, wet machines. However, when machines lose their socially-determined usefulness, they are thrown on to a junk heap.

Besides, if all of our choices and behaviors are entirely controlled by biochemical laws, then punishment is not a matter of justice. Instead, it is merely a matter of the "tyranny of the majority." However, the Bible *always* assumes that we indeed have responsible choices to make. As Joshua had commanded Israel: "Choose this day whom you will serve." (Joshua 24:15)

JUSTICE

Justice was formerly administered according to the guilt of the individual. Now, in ever-increasing instances, justice is becoming a matter of group-guilt relative to sex, sexual practice, color, race, religion…and to social appraisal of who has been oppressed. This new version of "justice" can only lead to distrust and division.

SAMN—the secularists, atheists, materialists and naturalists— have no basis upon which to believe in an objective good and bad, or what is just and unjust, or what is right and wrong. These are now regarded as socially-evolving ideas, relative to each society. Therefore, we now lack any objective standards upon which we may judge any culture or anyone within a culture. Even a Hitler would be exempt from censure according to the new rules of the game. In contrast, humanity has always recognized objective standards of justice by which the guilty party is to be judged for his criminality, while the innocent are to be protected:

- Be subject for the Lord's sake to every human institution, whether it be to the emperor as supreme, or to governors as sent by him to punish those who do evil and to praise those who do good. (1 Peter 2:13-14)

OBJECTIVE MORAL LAW AND MORALITY

Once SAMN rejects the Law-Giver, there remains no basis for objective laws or principles. Laws, therefore, must be humanly-created. This represents a major shift from principled Biblical thinking to a pragmatic cost/benefit analysis. However, human history has shown us that such thinking inevitably favors those in power, who value their own cost/benefit analysis above all others. One prime example of this is the way that the United States

Congress regularly votes to give itself a raise, including generous benefits vastly superior to those of most ordinary American citizens. In contrast:

- When he [the king] takes the throne of his kingdom, he is to write for himself on a scroll a copy of this law, taken from that of the priests, who are the Levites. It is to be with him, and he is to read it all the days of his life so that he may learn to revere the LORD his God and follow carefully all the words of this law and these decrees *and not consider himself better than his brothers* and turn from the law to the right or to the left…(Deuteronomy 17:18-20)

MEANING AND PURPOSE OF LIFE

SAMN has no rational basis to believe in the objective existence of a meaning and a purpose for life. Since the cosmos was not created with any purpose in mind, we are left to fend for ourselves…to create our own meaning and purpose.

So then, how can we account for the fact that so many secularists, atheists, materialists and naturalists do morally good things? Because doing such things produces benefits for them! But once the benefits diminish, the temptation to do what will produce more benefits will arise. A pragmatic, cost/benefit analysis will then be unable to ward off more self-serving temptations. Altruistic endeavors will be a casualty of this analysis and will tend to fall by the wayside, quickly.

SCIENCE

Instead of the devotion of science to a search for the truth, science has adopted a narrow, secularized stance—the search for a natural understanding. However, it would be good for us to remember that the emergence and flowering of modern science is a product of the

Christian West. British scientist Robert Clark summed it up this way:

- However we may interpret the fact, scientific development has only occurred in Christian culture. The ancients had brains as good as ours. In all civilizations—Babylonia, Egypt, Greece, India, Rome, Persia, China and so on—science developed to a certain point and then stopped. It is easy to argue speculatively that, perhaps, science might have been able to develop in the absence of Christianity, but in fact, it never did. And no wonder. For the non-Christian world believed that there was something ethically wrong about science. In Greece, this conviction was enshrined in the legend of Prometheus, the fire-bearer and prototype scientist who stole fire from heaven, thus incurring the wrath of the gods.[2]

❖ ❖ ❖

All of the principles I have written about in this chapter find their objective support in the Biblical revelation. However, in the absence of any rational basis for these principles, secularists, atheists, materialists and naturalists are counseled to *make-believe* that these principles do indeed have an objective existence. Why? Because all of these principles are pragmatically necessary. Therefore, we are supposed to believe in free will—not because it really exists—*but because we rationally need it to exist*. We must also make-believe that there is actually a right and a wrong, a just and an unjust. We must make believe in human rights and primacy. Finally, we must make believe that some behaviors are wrong—simply because of pragmatic concerns. And the outcome of this foolishness? Cynicism and alienation!

Playing make-believe is out-of-sync with reality. Doesn't this disqualify the validity of the worldview of secularism, atheism, materialism and naturalism?

Chapter 34

The German philosopher, Friedrich Nietzsche, foresaw the demise of Christianity and the inevitable consequences of the rejection of Biblical constraints. Consequently, he held the "common man" in contempt because they rejoiced at this "death of God"…yet they were unable to fathom its cost. Accordingly, Donna Gunderson Hailson has written:

- More than a century ago, Friedrich Nietzsche suggested that the idea of God was dead and, that if the world were to be without this sense of divine order and attaching moral principles, it would be left with nihilism—no meaning, no purpose, no intrinsic value. Nietzsche attributed two central principles of Western civilization to Christianity: all people are created equal and in the image of God, that our lives have moral worth and that we share the rights to life, liberty and the pursuit of happiness. Nietzsche's warning was that none of these values would make sense without the background moral framework against which they were formulated. A post-Christian West, he argued, would have to go back to the ethical drawing board for a reconsideration of its values.[3]

I do not think that nihilism is the worst thing that could happen to us. Instead, even worse is the vacuum created by our rejection of God and the feverish attempt to find an alternative substitute which does not exist. In our day, what I am referring to are socially constructed values that can only be maintained by coercion rather than reason. In fact, the coercion can be vicious. With ever-increasing frequency, we are seeing the public disparaging of people who do not tow the "party-line." Reputations are being trashed and jobs lost. Citing just one example among many, the issue that could ruin a life is the belief that gender is biologically determined.

THE LIMITS OF PROOFS, EVEN OF MIRACLES

CHAPTER SUMMARY

C.S. Lewis argued that our worldview commitments prevent us from interpreting the evidence correctly. At the heart of this is our love of the darkness and our hatred of God's light.

When a militant atheist feels as if he has been backed up against a wall, he pulls out his trump-card: "Well, prove that God exists."

Don't be tempted by the bait. You will never be able to provide proof that a "card-carrying" atheist would accept. Instead, you might ask him: "What type of evidence would you find satisfying?"

He might respond, "If God exists, I want him to appear to me right now." However, not even such a miraculous appearance would make any difference to him. The late author and scholar, C.S. Lewis, recounts an interesting story:

- One person...claimed to have seen a ghost. It was a woman; and the interesting thing is that she disbelieved in the immortality of the soul before seeing the ghost and still disbelieves after having seen it. She thinks it was a hallucination.[1]

From this, Lewis concluded that "seeing is *not* believing." Why not?

- Whatever experiences we may have, we shall not regard them as miraculous if we already hold a philosophy which excludes the supernatural...We can always say we have been the victims of an illusion; if we disbelieve in the supernatural this is what we always shall say.[2]

Lewis then took this principle a step further:

- For let us make no mistake. If the end of the world appeared in all the literal trappings of the Apocalypse, if the modern materialist saw with his own eyes the heavens rolled up and the great white throne appearing, if he had the sensation of being himself hurled into the Lake of Fire, he would continue forever, in that lake itself, to regard this experience as an illusion and to find the explanation of it in psycho-analysis, or cerebral pathology.[3]

If the facts do not agree with our worldview, then the facts are easily ignored. Years ago at a family get-together, we—all of us present being either agnostic or atheistic—stood spell-bound for an hour at the sight of our two little-girl-cousins doing the Ouija Board. The girls were spooked by this Board, and it required a lot of adult persuasion and reassurance to get them to perform. Here are the facts about which we all agreed:

✓ Even blindfolded, the disk scurried around the Board, spelling out adult words with adult thoughts and sensibilities. All of us ruled out any possibility of deception on the part of the girls.

✓ The girls came up with answers that they were naturally incapable of knowing.

✓ None of us suspected that what we were viewing was illusory or the product of a hallucination. We were all seeing and hearing the same things, over the time-span of at least an hour.

Over the years, I have asked my skeptical family about what they had concluded, based on what they had seen. None had a natural explanation, nor did anyone try to ascribe what they had seen to a hallucination. And yet, this event made no impact on their worldview. As Lewis declared, "seeing is not believing," even when no alternative explanation is available.

I don't think that we can easily comprehend humanity's hatred of the facts. Nor can we fathom the depth of our own aversion to the light of truth. However, spiritual blindness is the consistent revelation of Scripture. Jesus also pronounced this same verdict against humanity:

- "And this is the judgment: the light has come into the world, and people loved the darkness rather than the light because their works were evil. For everyone who does wicked things hates the light and does not come to the light, lest his works should be exposed." (John 3:19-20, ESV)

Apart from the grace of God, we are lovers of darkness and have been taken captive by what we love:

- And the Lord's servant must not be quarrelsome but kind to everyone, able to teach, patiently enduring evil, correcting his opponents with gentleness. God may perhaps grant them repentance leading to a knowledge of the truth, and they may come to their senses and escape from the snare of the devil, after being captured by him to do his will. (2 Timothy 2:24-26)

We have been imprisoned by Satan. But this prison does not require chains and bars—we are willing captives. Because we are enemies of the truth (Romans 5:8-10), we require more than proper argumentation, love, or even miracles to secure our freedom. God has to give us a new heart and mind so that we can receive the truth, "come to [our] senses," and escape our bondage.

If we fail to grasp the fact that this is a supernatural battle, we will become very frustrated with both the skeptics we encounter and our own efforts at evangelism. We need to remember that the battle for the mind is not primarily waged against flesh and blood, but against the devil himself:

- Put on the whole armor of God, that you may be able to stand against the schemes of the devil. For we do not wrestle against flesh and blood, but against the rulers, against the authorities, against the cosmic powers over this present darkness, against the spiritual forces of evil in the heavenly places. (Ephesians 6:11-12)

When we perceive the far-reaching, cosmic dimensions of the battle in which we are engaged, we realize on Whom we must rely.

But this does not mean that we are innocent pawns in this conflict. Instead, we have willingly and culpably given ourselves over to the powers of darkness:

- Now this I say and testify in the Lord, that you must no longer walk as the Gentiles do, in the futility of their minds. They are darkened in their understanding, alienated from the life of God because of the ignorance that is in them, due to their hardness of heart. They have become callous and have given themselves up to sensuality, greedy to practice every kind of impurity. (Ephesians 4:17-19)

Why have they given themselves over to the darkness? *Because of "their hardness of heart."* We have rejected God in favor of our own desires. As a result of this, God has given us up to the blinding influence of these desires (Romans 1:24, 26, 28; Psalm 81:12). Consequently, the Lord Himself must rescue us from unbelief.

When the Lord performs this miracle in our lives, bringing us out of the darkness and into His light, we become important participants in His plan. We are those who are loving, patient, humble, and respectful. We provide answers for those who are skeptical. It is my prayer that this book may contribute something of usefulness and value to our endeavors on the Lord's behalf.

CITATIONS

Chapter 1

1. Malone, Bruce A. *Search for the Truth. 2003.*

2. Lewis, C.S. *God in the Dock.* Grand Rapids, Michigan: Wm. B. Eerdman's Publishing Co., 2014, p. 173.

Chapter 2

1. https://www.revelationmovement.com/why-christianity-lost-america/

2. Ibid.

3. Ibid.

4. Schmidt, Alvin J. *How Christianity Changed the World.* Grand Rapids, Michigan: Zondervan, 20001, p. 190.

5. https://www.revelationmovement.com/why-christianity-lost-america/

6. Ibid.

7. Schmidt, pp. 243-244.

Chapter 3

1. Clark, Robert. *Christian Belief and Science: A Reconciliation and a Partnership.* London, English Universities Press, 1960; quoted by Henry F. Shaefer, p. 14.

2. http://mannsword.blogspot.com/2010/03/naturalism-vs-supernaturalism.html

3. http://mannsword.blogspot.com/2009/11/science-and-christianity.html

4. Guiness, Os. *The Journey*. Colorado Springs, CO: NavPress, 2001, p. 27.

5. Richard Dawkins vs. John Lennox, "The God Delusion Debate," published 5 February 2017 by Fixed Point Foundation.
https://www.youtube.com/watch?v=zF5bPI92-5o

6. *Look Magazine*. 16 January 1962, p. 46.

7. Gray, Sir James. *Science Today*. 1961, p. 21.

8. Leisola, Matti and Witt, Jonathan. *Heretic: One Scientist's Journey from Darwin to Design*. Seattle: Discovery Institute Press, 2018.

9. Ibid.

10. Ibid.

Chapter 4

1. https://quotefancy.com/quote/1507759/Ian-Stewart-Chaos-is-lawless-behavior-governed-entirely-by-law

2. Sagan, Carl. "Life" in *Encyclopedia Britannica: Macropaedia,* 1974 ed., pp. 893-894.

3. https://www.goodreads.com/quotes/344597-in-the-discoveries-of-science-the-harmony-of-the-spheres

4. Futuyma, Douglas. *Evolutionary Biology*, 3rd Ed. Sinauer, 1998, p. 5.

5. http://ubcgcu.org/2013/03/05/mind-expanding-quotes-on-fine-tuning/

6. Ibid.

CITATIONS

7. Ibid.

8. Ibid.

9. Geisler, Norman L. *If God, Why Evil? A New Way to Think About the Question.* Bloomington, Minnesota: Bethany House Publishers, 2011.

10.
http://www.forananswer.org/Top_Ath/Exclusive%20Interview%20 with%20Former%20Atheist%20Antony%20Flew.pdf

11. Flew, Antony. *There is a God: How the World's Most Notorious Atheist Changed His Mind.* 2007 Kindle edition, p. 75.

Chapter 5

1. Custance, Arthur C. and Travis, Lee Edward. *The Mysterious Matter of Mind.* Christian Free University Curriculum, 1979, pp. 95-96.

2. Strobel, Lee. *The Case for a Creator.* Grand Rapids, Michigan: Zondervan, 2004, p. 258.

3. Glynn, Patrick. *God: The Evidence.* Prima Lifestyles, 1997, pp. 103-104.

4. Strobel, p. 251.

5. http://www.express.co.uk/news/science/670781/There-IS-life-after-DEATH-Scientists-reveal-shock-findings-from-groundbreaking-study

6. Ibid.

CITATIONS

Chapter 6

1. Donegan, Alan. *Reflections on Philosophy and Religion.* Oxford University Press, New York: 1999, p. 24.

2. Tolstoy, Leo. *War and Peace.* Minneola, New York: Dover Publications, Inc., 2017.

3. Dennett, Daniel C. *Consciousness Explained.* Boston: Back Bay Books, 1991.

4. Harris, Sam. *Free Will.* New York: Free Press, 2012.

5. Hillman, James. *The Soul's Code: In Search of Character and Calling.* New York: Random House, 2017, p. 6.

Chapter 7

1. http://www.express.co.uk/news/science/670781/There-IS-life-after-DEATH-Scientists-reveal-shock-findings-from-groundbreaking-study

2. https://www.mdpi.com/2076-0787/4/4/775

3. https://nyaspubs.onlinelibrary.wiley.com/doi/abs/10.1111/nyas.12582

4. Van Lommel P, van Wees R, Meyers V, Elfferich I. (2001) "Near-Death Experience in Survivors of Cardiac Arrest: A Prospective Study in the Netherlands" in *The Lancet*, December 15; 358(9298):2039–45.

5. Glynn, Patrick. *God: The Evidence.* Prima Lifestyles, 1997, pp. 103-104.

6. http://www.ukapologetics.net/07/mindandbody.htm

CITATIONS

7. Lewontin, Richard. Review of *The Demon-Haunted World*, by Carl Sagan. In *New York Review of Books*, January 9, 1997.

8. Todd, Scott C. "A View from Kansas on the Evolution Debates." *Nature* (vol. 401. September 30, 1999), p. 423.

9. D'Souza, Dinesh. *Life After Death: The Evidence.* Washington, D.C.: Regnery Publishing, Inc., 2009, p. 108.

10. Koestler, Arthur. *Ghost in the Machine.* London: Hutchinson, 1967, p. 203.

11. Strobel, Lee. *The Case for a Creator*. Grand Rapids, Michigan: Zondervan, 2004, p. 258. (J. P. Moreland, interviewed by Lee Strobel.)

12. Ritchie, Mark Andrew. *Spirit of the Rainforest: A Yanomam Shaman's Story.* Island Lake Press, 2000, p. 238.

13. Ankerberg, John, and Weldon, John. *The Facts on Spirit Guides.* Eugene, Oregon: Harvest House Publishers, 1988, p. 27.

14. Ibid., p. 37.

15. Ibid., p. 39.

16. Ibid., pp. 39-40.

17. Ibid., p. 40.

18. Ibid., p. 40.

19. Frank, Patrick. "Whence the 'Noble Savage.'" *Skeptic Magazine,* Vol 9, #1, 2001, pp. 54-60.

20. Ankerberg, John and Weldon, John, p. 38.

CITATIONS

Chapter 8

1. https://realphysics.blogspot.com/2010/10/

2. https://www.brainyquote.com/quotes/albert_einstein_125369

3. Hawking, Stephen, and Mlodinow, Leonard. *The Grand Design.* New York: Bantam Books, 2010.

4. http://ubcgcu.org/2013/03/05/mind-expanding-quotes-on-fine-tuning

5. Ibid.

6. Hawking, Stephen, and Mlodinow, Leonard.

7. Ibid.

8. Ibid.

9. Folger, Tim. "The Multiverse Theory." *Discover Magazine*, December 2008.

Chapter 9

1. Malone, Bruce and Von Vett, Julie. *Have You Considered: Evidence Beyond A Reasonable Doubt.* Google Books, 2017.

2. Ibid.

3. Ibid.

Chapter 10

1. Keller, Timothy. *The Reason for God.* New York: Dutton, 2008, pp. 137-138.

CITATIONS

2. Lewis, C.S. *Present Concerns*, New York: HarperOne, 1986, p. 76.

Chapter 11

1. Hawking, Stephen and Penrose, Roger. *The Nature of Space and Time*. Princeton, New Jersey: Princeton University Press, 1996, p. 20.

2. Hawking, Stephen. *Brief Answers to the Big Questions*. New York: Bantam Books, 2018, p. 43.

3. Russell, Bertrand. Edited by Edwards, Paul. *Why I Am Not a Christian*. New York: A Touchstone Book, 1957, p. 7.

4. Geisler, Norman L. and Turek, Frank. *I Don't Have Enough Faith to Be an Atheist*. Wheaton, Illinois: Crossway Books, 2004, p. 85.

5. Jensen, Peter. *The Revelation of God*. Downer's Grove, Illinois: InterVarsity Press, 2002, p. 115.

6. https://www.facebook.com/UnlockingTheMysteriesOfCreation/posts/264595001881319   4

7. Jastrow, Robert. *God and the Astronomers*. New York: W.W. Norton, 1992, p. 107.

Chapter 12

1. Lindsay, Ronald A. "How Morality Has the Objectivity that Matters—Without God." Essay in *Free Inquiry,* Volume 34, No. 5, August/September 2014.

2. Ibid.

3. Ibid.

4. Noebel, David A. *Understanding the Times.* Quote from "Humanist Manifesto II." Summit Press, 2006, p. 237.

5. *Christian Research Journal,* Vol. 33, No. 2, 2010, p. 32.

6. Noebel, p. 237.

7. Lindsay.

8. https://theoriq.com/en/articles/moral-education-is-a-universal-thing-1228

9. Ibid.

10. Wright, Karen. *Psychology Today.* May 2008, p. 76.

Chapter 13

1. Kreeft, Peter and Tacelli, Ronald. *Handbook of Christian Apologetics.*

2. Ibid.

3. Ibid.

4. Ibid.

5. Hillman, James. *The Soul's Code: In Search of Character and Calling.* New York: Random House, 2017, p. 6.

Chapter 14

1. DeYoung, D. B. *Astronomy and the Bible: Questions and Answers.* United States: Baker Books, 2000, pp. 137- 138.

2. https://philosophydungeon.weebly.com/analogy.html

3. Nadis, Steve. "Starting Point." *Discover,* September 2013.

CITATIONS

Chapter 16

1. Walia, Arjun. "The Illusion of Matter: Our Physical Material World Isn't Really Physical At All." Article in *Collective Evolution,* 5 December 2013.

2. Henry, R. C. "The Mental Universe." Article in *Nature* 436:29, 2005, p. 14.

3. Kushiner, James A. "Is a Cosmic Counter-Revolution in the Making?" Article in *Salvo*, #32, Spring 2015, p. 64.

Chapter 17

1. McGrath, Alister. "The Twilight of Atheism." Ingersoll, Robert G., quoted from article in *Christianity Today.* 28 February 2005.

2. https://biblescienceguy.wordpress.com/2011/07/23/13-fox-in-the-hen-house-jesus-or-giberson/

3. Lewis, C.S. *Mere Christianity.* New York: MacMillan, 1960, p. 31.

4. https://newcriterion.com/issues/2006/3/what-auden-believed

5. Keller, Timothy. *The Reason for God.* New York: Dutton, 2008, p. 75.

6. Ibid., p. 75.

7. Ibid.

8. Ibid., p. 78.

9. https://www.facebook.com/152173524843663/posts/hell-is-the-greatest-monument-to-human-freedom-cs-lewis/815699328491076/

10. Keller, pp. 78-79.

11. Ibid., p. 79.

Chapter 19

1. https://users.drew.edu/jlenz/whynot.html

2. Ibid.

Chapter 21

1. Guiness, Os. *The Journey*. Colorado Springs, CO: NavPress, 2001, p. 136.

2. Himmelfarb, Gertrude, ed. *The Spirit of the Age: Victorian Essays*. (Excerpt taken from Nietzsche. *Twilight of the Idols*.) New Haven: Yale University Press, 2007, p. 17.

3. Farrow, Douglas. *Ascension and Ecclesia: On the Significance of the Ascension for Ecclesiology and Christian Cosmology*. Edinburgh: T and T Clark, 1999, p. 190.

4. Ibid.

5. https://www.goodreads.com/quotes/7322711-if-we-present-a-man-with-a-concept-of-man

6. Weikart, Richard. *From Darwin to Hitler: Evolutionary Ethics, Eugenics, and Racism in Germany*. New York: Palgrave Macmillan, 2004.

7. Ibid.

8. https://www.goodreads.com/quotes/145498-god-does-not-die-on-the-day-when-we-cease

CITATIONS

9. Nietzsche, Friedrich. *The Gay Science.* New York: Vintage Books, 1974. Section 125, "The Madman."

10. Leff, Arthur. Excerpt from Duke Law Journal, 1979.

Chapter 22

1. Guiness, Os. *The Journey.* Colorado Springs, CO: NavPress, 2001, p. 119.

2. Glynn, Patrick. *God: The Evidence.* Prima Lifestyles, 1997, p. 64.

3. Ibid., p. 61.

4. https://www.azquotes.com/quote/1447225

5. Russell, Bertrand. Edited by Edwards, Paul. *Why I Am Not a Christian.* New York: A Touchstone Book, 1957.

6. Guiness, p. 106.

7. MacLaine, Shirley. *It's All in the Playing.* New York: Bantam Doubleday Dell, 1991.

8. https://en.wikipedia.org/wiki/Shirley_MacLaine

Chapter 23

1. https://www.brainyquote.com/quotes/c_s_lewis_162523

2. Guiness, Os. *The Journey.* Colorado Springs, CO: NavPress, 2001.

3. Ibid.

4. Frankl, Viktor E. *Man's Search for Meaning.* Boston: Beacon Press, 1992.

5. Karp, David A. *Speaking of Sadness*. Oxford: Oxford
University Press, 1996, p. 191.

Chapter 24

1. Aaronson, Lauren. "Make a Gratitude Adjustment." *Psychology Today.* March/April 2006.

2. Guinness, Os. *The Journey: Our Quest for Faith and Meaning.* Colorado Springs, CO: NavPress, 2001, p. 38.

3. Solomon, Andrew. *The Noonday Demon: An Atlas of Depression*. New York: Scribner, 2001, book jacket.

4. Ibid., p. 430.

5. Peck, M. Scott. *Further Along the Road Less Traveled.* New York: Simon and Schuster, 1993, p. 24.

6. Solomon, p. 137.

7. Wright, Karen. "Dare to Be Yourself." *Psychology Today.* May/June 2008: p. 72.

8. Ibid., p. 75.

9. Taylor, Shelley E. *Positive Illusions: Creative Self-Deception and the Healthy Mind*. New York: Basic Books, 1989, p. 46.

10. Fitzpatrick, Elyse M. "The Gospel Cure." *Tabletalk.* March 2008, pp. 15–16.

11. Wright, p. 76.

12. Dawkins, Richard. *The God Delusion.* New York: Houghton Mifflin Company, 2006, p. 221.

CITATIONS

13. Noebel, David A., *Understanding the Times*, abridged ed. Colorado Springs, CO: Association of Christian Schools International, 1995, p. 237.

14. Guinness, p. 39.

15. Hillman, James. *The Soul's Code.* New York: Random House, 1996, pp. 5–6.

16. Guinness.

17. Deikman, Arthur J. *The Observing Self: Mysticism and Psychotherapy.* Boston: Beacon Press, 1982, pp. 4–5.

18. Russell, Bertrand. *"A Free Man's Worship,"* in *Why I Am Not a Christian*, quoted in Guinness, p. 105.

19. Ibid., p. 106.

20. Bradshaw, John. *Homecoming: Reclaiming and Championing Your Inner Child.* New York: Bantam House, 1990, p. 67.

21. Ibid., p. 93.

22. Gottman, John M. *The Seven Principles for Making Marriage Work.* New York: Three Rivers Press, 1999, p. 24.

23. Hendrix, Harville. *Getting the Love You Want: A Guide for Couples.* New York: HarperPerennial, 1990, p. 119.

24. Crabb, Larry. *The Marriage Builder.* Grand Rapids, MI: Zondervan, 1992, p. 12.

CITATIONS

Chapter 25

1. Mangalwadi, Vishal. *Truth and Transformation: A Manifesto for Ailing Nations.* Seattle, Washington: YWAM Publishing, 2009.

2. Ibid.

3. Ibid.

4. Mangalwadi, Vishal. *The Book that Made your World.* Nashville, Tennessee: Thomas Nelson, 2011, p. 108.

5. Ibid., p. 109.

6. Ibid., pp. 101-102.

7. Ibid., p. 112.

8. Ibid.

9. Ibid.

10. Ibid.

11. Woodberry, Robert. *Christianity Today.* Jan/Feb 2014, p. 39.

12. Newcombe, Jerry. *The Unstoppable Jesus Christ.* Hermosa Beach, California: Creator's Publishing, 2016.

Chapter 26

1. Schmidt, Alvin. *How Christianity Changed the World.* Grand Rapids, Michigan: Zondervan, 2001, pp. 128-29.

2. *Epistles of Julian,* p. 49.

CITATIONS

3. Warfield, B.B. *The Works of Benjamin B. Warfield.* Grand Rapids, Michigan: Baker Book House, 2003.

4. Schmidt, p. 137.

5. Ibid., p. 138.

6. Ibid.

7. Watson, Frank Dekker. *Charity Organization Movement in the United States: Study in American Philanthropy.* New York: Macmillan, 1922, p. 12.

8. Schmidt, p. 138.

9. Hayes, Carlton. *Christianity and Western Civilization.* The Raymond Fred West Memorial Lectures at Stanford University, 1954, p. 56.

10. Schmidt, pp. 166-167.

11. Ibid., p. 148.

12. Garrison, Fielding. *Introduction to the History of Medicine,* 1921, p. 118.

13. Schmidt, pp. 166-167.

14. Ibid., p. 131.

15. Stamp, Josiah. *Christianity and Economics.* Facsimile Publisher, 1939, p. 69.

16. Stark, Rodney. *The Victory of Reason: How Christianity Led to Freedom, Capitalism, and Western Success.* New York: Random House, 2005, xi.

17. Mangalwadi, Vishal. *The Book that Made your World.* Nashville, Tennessee: Thomas Nelson, 2011, p. 311.

18. Ibid., p. 312.

19. Ibid.

20. Ibid., p. 314.

21. Ibid.

Chapter 27

1. Sampson, Philip J. *6 Modern Myths about Christianity and Western Civilization.* Downer's Grove, IL: IVP Press, 2001.

2. Ibid., p. 100.

3. Tucker, Ruth A. *From Jerusalem to Irian Jaya.* Grand Rapids, Michigan: Zondervan, 1983, p. 140.

4. Sampson, p. 101.

5. Ibid., p. 102.

6. Ibid., p. 103.

7. Ibid., pp. 103-104.

8. Neill, Stephen. *History of Christian Missions.* London: Penguin Books, 1986, p. 355.

9. Tucker, p. 140.

10. Giberson, Karl. *Saving Darwin: How to Be a Christian and Believe in Evolution.* New York: HarperOne, 2008.

11. Tucker, p. 111.

12. Ibid.

CITATIONS

13. Sampson, pp. 109-110.

14. Ibid., p. 110.

15. Ibid., p. 111.

16. Ibid.

17. Ibid., p. 98.

18. Ibid.

19. Yancy, Philip. *Christianity Today.* Nov. 2010, pp. 32-33.

20. Yung, Hwa. *Christianity Today.* Nov. 2011, p. 44.

21. Ibid.

22. Ibid.

23. Ibid.

Chapter 28

1. Stark, Rodney. *The Victory of Reason: How Christianity Led to Freedom, Capitalism, and Western Success.* New York: Random House, 2006, xi.

2. Ibid., p. 12.

3. Ibid., p. 26.

4. Ibid., p. 27.

5. Ibid., pp. 77-78.

6. Ibid., p. 233.

7. Parris, Matthew. Essay entitled: "As an atheist, I truly believe Africa needs God." Reposted from: http://www.timesonline.co.uk/tol/comment/columnists/matthew_parris/article5400568.ece (originally published by the London Times 27 Dec. 2008, and reposted 07 Jan 2009 in The Richard Dawkins Foundation's official website).

8. Ibid.

9. Swain, Carol M. *Be the People: A Call to Reclaim America's Faith and Promise.* Nashville: Thomas Nelson, 2011, p. 31.

10. Stark, p. 235.

11. https://ionainstitute.ie/christianity-the-reason-for-wests-success-say-the-chinese/

Chapter 29

1. De Tocqueville, Alexis. *Democracy in America.* Chicago: University of Chicago Press, 2000.

2. Gaus, Gerald F., quoting Robert Bellah. *Social Philosophy.* London: Routledge, 2015, p. 42.

Chapter 30

1. Mangalwadi, Vishal. *The Book that Made your World.* Nashville: Thomas Nelson, 2011, p. 259.

2. Ibid., pp. 260-261.

3. Ibid., p. 262.

4. Ibid.

5. Ibid.

CITATIONS

6. DeMoss, Nancy Leigh. *The Rebirth of America*. Arthur S. Demoss Foundation, 1986, p. 64.

7. Darwin, Charles. *The Works of Charles Darwin*, Vol. 3, Part Two. Edited by Barrett, Paul H. and Freeman, R. B. New York: New York University Press, 1987, p. 386.

Chapter 31

1. Weaver, George M. *The Significant Life.* Rapid City, South Dakota: CrossLink Publishing, 2014, p. 7.

2. Ibid., p. 58.

3. Ibid., p. 44.

4. Ibid., p. 45.

5. Ibid., p. 47.

6. Huxley, Aldous. *Ends and Means.* New York: Routledge, 2017, pp. 270, 273.

Chapter 33

1. http://www.nytimes.com/2007/11/20/health/research/20deni.html?pagewanted=all&_r=0

2. https://ssa.uchicago.edu/research-journal-many-faces-denial

3. Taylor, Shelley. *Positive Illusions.* Basic Books, 1989, p. 46.

4. http://imaginefirestone.org/wp-content/uploads/2010/02/RethinkingSelf-Esteem.pdf

5. Lewontin, Richard. Review of *The Demon-Haunted World*, by Carl Sagan. In *New York Review of Books*, 9 January 1997.

6. Todd, Scott C., "A View from Kansas on the Evolution Debates," *Nature,* Vol. 401. September 30, 1999, p. 423.

Chapter 34

1. https://www.goodreads.com/quotes/3494-but-recently-i-have-learned-from-discussions-with-a-variety

2. Clark, Robert E. D. *Christian Belief and Science*, quoted by Henry F. Schaefer. Philadelphia: Fortress Press, 1960, p. 14.

3. Hailson, Donna Gunderson. *The Rockery: Theology, Nature, and the Arts as Spiritual Ambassadors for the Christian Faith,* e-magazine, 7 August 2016.

Chapter 35

1. Lewis, C.S. *God in the Dock*. Grand Rapids, Michigan: Wm. B. Eerdmans, 2014, p. 8.

2. Ibid., p. 8.

3. Ibid., pp. 8-9.